When Your Family's Lost a Loved One

finding

hope

together

DAVID & NANCY GUTHRIE

To: Lawson family

Our prayer is that this Book would be another step in the healing process!
May You sense God's Presence as You Read.

Rob & Sheila

"After my wife and all four children drowned in a flash flood, I held onto the Guthries' words of hope that immediately soothed my shattered soul. Like me, you will instantly connect with David and Nancy. Their honesty and empathy will validate, articulate, and resonate with your pain. Their heartfelt words in this book will give you the inspiration and godly direction you desperately long for on your journey through your valley of grief. God will indeed speak through these pages to help restore your wounded soul."

—ROBERT ROGERS
Founder, Mighty in the Land Ministry
and author, *Into the Deep*

"I wish I'd had a copy of this book when I first got home from the jungle after losing my husband, Martin. After being held captive by the Abu Sayyaf for a year in the Philippines, he was killed in the gun battle that led to my rescue.

"God, in His incredible goodness and kindness, brought Nancy Guthrie into my life soon after my rescue. She acted as my publicist as I was thrust into the media spotlight after my return to the U.S. She took me to interviews, sat with me as they did my makeup, coached me on what was coming up—all the while encouraging me and talking with me about grief. I was listening. She had just been through much loss herself, and her words of counsel were invaluable!

"You may not be able to meet Nancy in person, but I am so glad that you can benefit from her and her husband's wisdom through this book. Thank you, David and Nancy, for being faithful to the Lord! Thank you for sharing your lives with those of us that are hurting! We are grateful for you."

—GRACIA BURNHAM
Author, *In the Presence of My Enemies*
and *To Fly Again: Surviving the Tailspins of Life*

"This is the first grief book you should read after the death of a family member. David and Nancy Guthrie guide you through the practical issues you need to face in the midst of your grief, while offering you hope that better days are ahead."

—STEVE GRISSOM

Founder, GriefShare

When Your Family's Lost a Loved One

When Your Family's Lost a Loved One

finding hope together

DAVID & NANCY GUTHRIE

Tyndale House Publishers, Inc., Carol Stream, Illinois

When Your Family's Lost a Loved One

Focus on the Family and the accompanying logo and design are federally registered trademarks of Focus on the Family, Colorado Springs, CO 80995.

A Focus on the Family book published by Tyndale House Publishers, Carol Stream, Illinois 60188

TYNDALE is a registered trademark of Tyndale House Publishers, Inc. Tyndale's quill logo is a trademark of Tyndale House Publishers, Inc.

Cover design: Jennifer Ghionzoli
Cover photo: Jimi Allen, copyright © by Focus on the Family. All rights reserved.
Author photo: Copyright © by Steve Wood. All rights reserved.

Library of Congress Cataloging-in-Publication Data
Guthrie, David.
    When your family's lost a loved one : finding hope together / David and Nancy Guthrie.
        p. cm.
    At head of title: Focus on the Family
    ISBN-13: 978-1-58997-480-7
    ISBN-10: 1-58997-480-8
  1. Grief—Religious aspects—Christianity. 2. Bereavement—Religious aspects—Christianity.
3. Consolation. I. Guthrie, Nancy. II. Title.
    BV4905.3.G88 2008
    248.8'66—dc22

                                                2007048849

Printed in the United States of America
1 2 3 4 5 6 7 / 14 13 12 11 10 09 08

Contents

*We lovingly dedicate this book to our son, Matt Guthrie.
You'll never know how happy it makes us
when you walk through the door.*

*While nothing has brought us as much sorrow
as losing your brother and sister,
nothing has brought us as much joy as these
18 years being your mom and dad.
We can hardly wait to see how God is going
to use you in this world to build His kingdom.*

Acknowledgments

We are grateful to Andrea Doering for suggesting we write this book, to Larry Weeden and the rest of the team at Focus on the Family for giving us the opportunity, and to John Duckworth for helping us say it a little better.

We have had such a sweet time sitting down with some of our friends and making new ones as we interviewed people for the Q&As in this book. We thank them not only for their time, but for their openness and honesty, and for their willingness to use the hurts in their lives to help others get through what they've gotten through.

As we've looked back on our own experience of getting our family through our losses, we are so grateful for the loving care we received from our church family at Christ Presbyterian Church in Nashville, Tennessee, for the limitless love of our parents, Claude and Ella Dee Jinks and Wink and Rita Guthrie, and for the companionship of so many friends who walked through such hard days with us.

Foreword

Little did I know when I became pastor of David and Nancy Guthrie and their son, Matt, that it would be my privilege to walk with them through the long, dark, and painful valley of losing two of their children.

The journey taken by the Guthrie family was a strange combination of great joy and deep sorrow. It was also a period of significant spiritual growth. The Guthries gained a deep understanding of how God graciously uses suffering to accomplish His purposes. They also came to appreciate as never before the blessing of being deeply rooted in the Body of Christ. They were loved well by their friends, and found within the Christian community the love and support all of us desperately need as we grope in the darkness with lots of fear, sadness, and a myriad of questions.

In the midst of their loss, I saw something beautiful happen. It wasn't that they were in denial over their loss or that they didn't struggle with fears or questions. Their pain and sadness was very real. But just as real was their response of faith, their determination to trust God with their losses, and their commitment to love each other well.

I have seen the Guthries emerge from the fire of extreme trial as refined gold. Their faith is deeper. Their spirits are sweeter. Their capacity to love and serve those who suffer is greater.

Somehow they look more like Jesus on this side of the valley than they did when they began the journey.

Since their own journey through the "valley of the shadow of death," David and Nancy have proven to be a blessing to untold thousands who are called to walk similar paths. I'm glad you have picked up this book because I believe you will be blessed by the insights they've gained from ministering to many, many people who have faced what you are facing in your loss.

As a pastor for over 40 years, I've walked with many families through very dark seasons of grief. I've stood with them at the grave. In that time I've seen many marriages and families struggle under the weight of sorrow, some never able to recover.

I pray that will not be your experience. I pray that you will gain insights and inspiration from this book, and that your family will emerge from your loss with joy for living and love for each other.

Charles McGowan
Brentwood, Tennessee
2007

Introduction

Welcome to the book you never wanted to read—the kind of book you never imagined you'd *need* to read.

But here you are, reeling from the death of your spouse or your child or another close family member. You're wondering if you'll always feel as much pain as you do now, wanting people to stop talking about your loss all the time yet fearing they'll forget, needing something to relieve the painful pressure you feel inside your chest.

Here you are needing hope. That's what we want to give you in this book—hope that your family can be healthy and whole, even as you face the future feeling so broken.

We're quick to tell you, however, that while we know the pain of loss, we haven't been exactly where you are today. No one has. Every loss in a family is unique.

We've faced the grave twice now, burying two of our three children. Our daughter, Hope, and our son, Gabriel, were born with a rare metabolic disorder called Zellweger Syndrome, which meant their lives were very difficult and very short.

Some people tell us they can't imagine going through what we've been through. But when we look around at the losses others experience, ours often feel small and insignificant in comparison.

So while we write about the losses of Hope and Gabriel throughout these chapters, it's not because our loss represents the epitome of pain. It's because we're hoping you'll find companionship in what we share—that you'll have moments of thinking, "I felt the same way!" or "I have the same question," or "Somebody said the same thing to me."

In addition to hope, we want to provide you with companionship.

Sometimes it can feel like nobody gets it, nobody really understands how hard everything about life feels at this point.

Because there are so many hard things about losing a family member that we haven't had to face personally, we've included interviews with people who've experienced losses different from our own—the loss of a wife, a husband, a child through suicide, a mother, a father, a sibling—who offer incredible insights. We've also included interviews with experts in education, psychiatry, parenting, and counseling on the topics of greatest concern to grieving families.

We hope you'll discover in this book that there are others who understand what it's like to face getting your family through the loss of a loved one. We trust you'll find hope and encouragement from those who've traveled this road before you.

In the years that have followed Hope's and Gabriel's deaths, and the publication of *Holding On to Hope* and *The One Year Book of Hope* (both published by Tyndale House Publishers), we've talked to and shed tears with lots of couples and individuals about their losses. There are, after all, things that only other people who've had a similar loss can understand, aren't there? The chapters that follow reflect the content of so many of those conversations—the very real relational, practical, emotional, and spiritual issues that grieving families wrestle with. This is what we'd share with you if we met you at Starbucks to hear about your loss and to tell you about ours.

We hope you'll grab a cup of coffee and pull up a chair. We'd like to talk openly and honestly about what it's going to take to get through this.

And we'd love to hear from you. You can contact us via www.nancyguthrie.com. We'd be honored to hear how you're doing as you get your family through the loss of your loved one.

David and Nancy Guthrie

Chapter One

How Are You?

Nancy

"How are you?"

It's the question everyone is asking you these days. You're grateful that people care—but it sometimes seems unanswerable, doesn't it?

"Fine" doesn't sound quite right. You may be functioning and perhaps even feeling better, but you know you're not "fine."

If you were honest, your answer might be one of these:

"I'm afraid."

"I'm disappointed."

"I'm relieved."

"I'm angry."

"I'm confused."

"I'm sad."

That was my answer for months after our daughter, Hope, died: "I'm sad."

I was deeply, devastatingly, pervasively sad. And I wanted those around me to give me time and space and permission to simply be sad.

IT'S OKAY TO BE SAD

Our culture is very uncomfortable with sadness. Unless they've lost someone close, most people don't understand how sorrowful simple aspects of daily life can be when you're grieving.

I remember the first time I went to the grocery store after my daughter, Hope, died. It was all I could do to get there, and I wept as I walked the aisles. Everywhere I looked I saw products I no longer needed to buy because she was gone. And it just seemed too ordinary a task; I was going back to life as usual, but without Hope. And that didn't feel right.

A few months later I went on a retreat with our choir. Standing up, I told everyone, "I haven't lost my faith. I'm not hopeless. I'm just sad. And I'm going to be sad for a while."

In those days, tears always seemed close to the surface. While I'd rarely cried before Hope, now a day rarely went by when there were no tears. There was so much pain inside that needed to find release.

Many people were afraid to say something to me about Hope, fearful it would cause me to think about her, adding to my pain. What they didn't know was that I was already thinking about her. When they spoke of her, it touched me, and my tears were a relief to me.

Recently a woman who'd lost her husband a few months earlier caught up with me after church. She told me she was crying all the time—at work, on her way home from work, and at home in the evenings. "What is wrong with me?" she asked.

"Wasn't your husband a significant part of your life?" I asked. "And wasn't his life precious and valuable?"

The answer, of course, was yes.

"Then isn't he worthy of a great sorrow?"

Before you can get on with your life, you will have to give way to grief.

For some, that may seem easy. For a while you may not *want* to feel better because the grief keeps the one you love close—even as the days and weeks seem to pull you away from the person you loved and still love.

But for others, sorrow feels like an enemy. Some people are afraid to cry—afraid that once they start, they may never be able to stop. Or they fear being unable to control when or where their tears come to the surface.

There's no need to rush ourselves through sadness or to avoid it altogether. Sorrow is not weakness, and tears do not reflect a lack of faith. God gives us the gift of tears to help us wash away the pain.

IT'S OKAY TO BE HAPPY

While sadness can be awkward, laughter can seem off-limits—or certainly inappropriate following the death of someone we love.

I remember being afraid that some people might think I was in complete denial—or worse, that I didn't really care about Hope—if I laughed out loud during her difficult life or following her death. And I remember the strange look I got from someone at a dinner the night before Gabriel's memorial service, when I asked a friend to tell a funny story and laughed heartily at it.

Sometimes we are afraid to laugh lest people think our pain has passed or that our sorrow has been a sham. But just as tears give vent to the deep sorrow we feel, laughter reveals that while grief may have a grip on us, it hasn't choked the life out of us.

Laughter takes some of the sting out of hurt. It gives us perspective and relieves the pressure. In fact, laughter actually increases the flow of endorphins, our bodies' naturally produced painkiller. It gives us a mini-vacation from our pain. And wouldn't you sometimes like to take a day off from your sorrow?

We know we've found a real friend when he or she is comfortable not only with our sadness in grief, but our laughter. And we're friends to ourselves when we allow ourselves to feel and express both.

IT'S OKAY TO HIDE

Many grieving people simply don't want to deal with others. They don't want to have awkward conversations and uncontrolled emotions. They want to be alone—to have time to think and reflect, and simply miss the person who is gone.

For some mysterious reason I've never been able to put my finger on, facing a crowd when you're grieving can be hard. Walking into church and other situations where so many people express their compassion can be emotionally overwhelming.

I remember feeling that I simply couldn't walk into the parents' orientation night at Matt's school a few months after Hope died. I feared my total identity was "that woman whose baby died," and with every acquaintance would come an emotionally draining conversation about Hope's death. Fewer people probably were thinking about me and my loss than I imagined, but the prospect of encountering so many I hadn't seen since Hope died during the summer overwhelmed me, so I stayed home.

Hiding, if only for a season, is acceptable when we're grieving. But hiding can become a habit, a way of life that robs us of healing relationships and a returning sense of normalcy.

It's Okay to Engage

Some people have the opposite problem—especially those who've been nursing a loved one through a long illness. Suddenly freed from patient care, they feel a little embarrassed by their sense of relief. They're ready to talk about their loved one and their grief and experience. They're comforted by the presence of others and sharing their memories.

We were blessed during Hope's life with people to talk to—including those who brought us meals. They were often surprised when we'd invite them to bring enough food to have dinner with us.

We had incredibly precious visits during those days. Meaningless conversations were rare. Instead, we talked about life and death and prayer and faith and eternity. It was a rich time, and we enjoyed engaging with people who cared.

Going through grief gives us a unique opportunity to bond with those we may barely have known before, if they dare to draw close to us in our pain. Conversations that go below the surface can become the foundation for new and deeper friendships that give us strength in the midst of sorrow.

It's Okay to Be Weak

The loss of someone we love reveals our very real vulnerability to sorrow and pain. At some point or another, most of us surrender to our weakness—and it can be very uncomfortable.

We may always have been in control, on top of things; now everything in our lives seems chaotic. The house is a mess, nobody has washed the clothes or paid the bills, and we can't seem to concentrate or carry on a reasonable conversation.

Grief reduces us to—or reveals to us—our neediness and weakness. Some of us have to learn how to receive help from others when we've always been self-sufficient. Others of us discover through the process of grief our own physical, emotional, and spiritual weakness that can no longer be covered up.

While this discovery can be unsettling, it's when we are weak that we are prepared to enter into God's strength. Jesus said, "Blessed are the poor in spirit" (Matthew 5:3). In other words, our weakness positions us as nothing else does to experience joy in God and connectedness with Him.

It's Okay to Be Strong

Some of us also discover in the midst of grief a strength we didn't know was there—in character, in mind and will, in commitment, in endurance, in faith. We have the opportunity to put God's strength on display through our weakness as He provides what we need in the midst of heartache and difficulty.

There are surely no simple answers to the question, "How are you?" when you're grieving. We can be sad but not devoid of joy and laughter, wanting to hide but willing to engage, weak in body and mind but strong in spirit.

Getting your family through the loss of your loved one requires making room for all these things in yourself and those around you. It requires allowing for completely conflicting emotions and inclinations. It requires a great deal of grace.

"BUT HOW ARE YOU REALLY DOING?"

David

Following close on the heels of "How are you?" is its requisite follow-up query:

"No . . . how are you . . . *really*?"

For many of us men, this is the dreaded, nails-on-the-chalkboard question. To us it implies one of the following:

(a) Your first response is never actually truthful, so now we'll press for the honest answer.

(b) You are clearly oblivious to your own feelings, and it will require somebody removing your blinders to let you see how you actually feel (and I've been appointed to that job).

(c) Your description of how you are is pathetic; here, we'll give you a second chance to come up with something better.

(d) All of the above.

What is it about this line of questioning from concerned friends that can make us so uncomfortable?

I think I know what it is for me. In the midst of my own pain and confusion, I suddenly also feel responsible to others to give an account for my progress. As the words of my reply come measured through my lips, I'm wondering if my report will be acceptable.

In a sense, I wouldn't be surprised if the questioner came back with, "Sorry, wrong answer. More hopeful confidence, please. Less feeling sorry for yourself. Less anger (or more)."

Most of us guys are "doers," and in the uncharted territory of grief we wonder if we're "doing it right." In general, we have no idea if we are or not; the seemingly suspicious questions hit us more as interrogation aimed at exposing us than as loving concern.

Interestingly, many of us find it much easier to answer the question, "How is your wife?" or "How are your kids?"

Our perspective on how family members are doing seems much clearer. We're observing them, we've talked things through with them. Though we're walking through deep and turbulent waters that are probably new to all of us, our senses may be more attuned to family members' daily condition than to our own. And generally we're more comfortable talking about them than about ourselves.

Another reason it's difficult to respond to this question is that most of the potential answers seem somehow off the mark.

"Fine."

"Good."

"I've been better."

"I'm surviving."

"I'm 32.7 percent better than I was last time you asked."

The responses poised on the ends of our tongues seem trite, glib, depressing, unbelievable, or insulting. Or they expose a lack of self-understanding to which we'd rather not admit.

I've found it helpful to tune my ear to hear a *different* question— or actually, not a question at all. As I slogged through the insecurity of grief with my family during our loss experiences, when someone asked, "How are you . . . really?" I began to translate it to mean, "I care about you."

It's that simple: "I am bold enough to ask this question because

I know you must be hurting. I know it must be very difficult. When I try to put myself in your shoes I can hardly imagine what it must be like. So I ask how you are. I really want to know, because I care about you."

Sure, I suspected that a few inquisitors were motivated more by an all-knowing superiority than by compassion: "I'll get you to dig down and tell me the dirty truth whether you want to or not!" Or, "I know grief, and I can tell by your superficial response that you're not really dealing with it yet."

But I chose to receive even those probings as gifts of concern. At least the interrogator cared enough to ask!

Eventually, I worked out simple, honest answers like these:

"It's very hard, but I'm doing well. Thank you so much for asking."

"This week was difficult because _____. Thanks so much for asking."

"Believe it or not, I'm great. Thanks for your prayers, and thanks so much for asking."

As I tried to respond graciously to probing questions, I saw that even though the process made me somewhat uncomfortable, it proved to be a blessing to the one who asked. This is a great arrangement, because it pays dividends for everybody. As Proverbs 11:25 (ESV) says, "Whoever brings blessing will be enriched, and one who waters will himself be watered."

Can you receive those sometimes-too-earnest inquiries that make you squirm or snarl as genuine gifts of love and concern? Can you see them as coming from friends who struggle to understand your situation and to know how they should respond?

Chances are that many people want to try to walk with you. Some want to help if they can; others just want to empathize. Receive them all as a gift from God, knowing that they care—really!

"And How Are You Doing As a Family?"

Nancy and David

When we think back to those early days of grief in our family, we real-ize that the process took a dramatically different shape for each of us.

Much of Nancy's emotion was wrapped up in disappointment that she wouldn't have a daughter who would look like her, talk like her, and grow up to be her friend in her old age.

David, on the other hand, felt the helplessness of a father who was unable to protect his daughter from the foreign invader—and a husband who couldn't make everything better for his sad wife.

While our son, Matt, couldn't articulate many of his thoughts and feelings at the time, we have to wonder: How does a sibling compete with the memory of a child who was never old enough or healthy enough to disobey or disappoint? How does he adjust to having parents who cry at the most inopportune times?

Perhaps the starting place for figuring out how your family is doing is to identify how the loss has affected each of you—to get outside your own thoughts and feelings to consider those of each family member.

That can be awkward, even intimidating. But it can also be re-warding and strengthening. You may wonder how your family will cope with the mixture of intense emotions and needs, but grief gives you an opportunity to go deeper with each other and grow closer to each other than you were before this loss. Grief does not have to drive you apart.

What will determine if you move away from each other or draw together, whether you emerge from this crisis broken, bitter, and divided or healthy, happy, and whole? It depends on whether you are willing to *identify* and *address* grief's impact on each member of your family—or if you choose to *ignore* and *avoid* it.

IGNORANCE IS BLISS?

It can seem more comfortable to ignore and avoid how grief is affecting your family as individuals and as a unit. Part of you may wish everyone would retreat to his or her own room and emotions and coping mechanisms rather than dealing with them head-on.

As humans who don't want to hurt, we have several ways to avoid feeling the pain of grief. Maybe you recognize one or more of the following in yourself or in other members of your family.

1. *Postpone*. We think that if we ignore it, it will just go away. So we push it out of our minds and put it on the shelf. We don't talk about it, hoping it will dissipate through neglect.

2. *Somaticize*. We become obsessed with our own health or lack thereof, using physical illness as a way to avoid our emotional pain.

3. *Minimize*. Using self-talk such as, "We weren't that close, anyway," we minimize the value of our relationship to the person who has died. By telling ourselves that our loss is not unique ("We all lose our parents at some point"), we try to convince ourselves that a common loss shouldn't hurt so much.

4. *Displace*. Rather than giving energy to our grief, we give it to blame, to righting a wrong, to making someone pay.

5. *Replace*. Many grieving people channel their energy into causes such as passing a law, starting a foundation, or pushing for research. A cause can be an excellent outlet for honoring someone who has died, but pouring energy into a cause before the work of grief is done can derail that important process.

6. *Spiritualize*. While we rest and rely on the promises of Scripture to bring us comfort in our grief, the truth of heaven does not take away the pain of loss.

Do you see yourself or other members of your family avoiding grief through any of these avenues? Grief is not to be avoided or ignored. It is not something you *get over* so you can *go on*; it is something you *get through*.

To help your family get through it, ignoring and avoiding won't work. You'll need to identify and address what each person in your family is thinking, feeling, and experiencing.

To Each His Own

It hurts when others ignore or dismiss your pain. But it can also be annoying when others want to examine and meddle in it. It's frustrating when they seem to suggest that you aren't grieving the "right" way, or on the "right" timetable.

What feels good is when those closest to us seek to understand our pain and even share it. This is what helps a family in grief grow close—as family members feel that others respect their individual losses as well as their individual expressions of grief.

It can be hard to find the energy to identify and understand what others in your family are feeling and experiencing when you feel overwhelmed by your own pain. But considering the pain of others is what draws out compassion and helps us to give each other space and grace.

Consider how various losses affect different family members in differing ways.

Loss of a Child

As a *parent,* you may be agonizing over the loss of your dreams for your child—what your child might have experienced and accomplished. You may be struggling with guilt over lost opportunities, missed cues, harsh words. While your spouse grieves, too, you may wonder why he or she seems so much sadder than you do—or doesn't seem sad at all. You may feel frustrated by his or her unwillingness to talk about your child—or to stop talking about your child. You may find yourself gripped by fear over losing another child, and tending to overprotect your other children.

Those surviving *children*, meanwhile, may feel lost—unsure of where they fit into your family structure without that brother or sister. They may suffer "survivor guilt" and feel compelled to please you. They could fear the future as they see their parents, who used to be in control, struggle to cope with everyday matters. They might even fear that they will die themselves.

Grandparents are sometimes the forgotten mourners. Our society underestimates the impact of the death of a grandchild. But grandparents not only lose a beloved grandchild; they also experience the pain of watching their child grieve the loss. And parents never stop wanting to protect their child from pain.

LOSS OF A SPOUSE

If you're the *husband* or *wife* who's lost your mate, you may be feeling a sense of desperation about the future—wondering how you'll get a meal on the table, pay the bills, make decisions on your own, endure the loneliness. You may have mixed feelings about whether or not you'll marry again; perhaps you can't stand the idea of spending the rest of your life alone, but it seems so hard to think about someone taking the place of your late spouse. You may find yourself leaning on one of your children for support, trying to turn him or her into a confidant. Perhaps you feel angry at your spouse for not seeking medical care earlier, angry with a doctor who misdiagnosed or mistreated, or angry with God.

Your *children* may be afraid of losing you, too. They may wonder who's going to teach them how to throw a ball, how to bake a cake, or what it means to be a man or woman. They may feel frustrated over being different from those at school who have a mom and dad, desperate to be "normal" like everybody else. They may long for "how it used to be" in the daily routines of your family.

As the *parent* of a child who has lost his or her spouse, you may find yourself feeling the load of increased responsibility for your grandchildren or the surviving spouse. Perhaps you want to help, but fear interfering. You may want to make everything better, and are frustrated that you can't. You may hurt over the pain you see in your grandchildren's eyes, and fear the long-term effects of this loss.

LOSS OF YOUR PARENT

As an adult *child*, you may be surprised by the intensity of your grief over losing your parent, not having anticipated what it would feel like for mom or dad to be there no longer as a resource. It may make you far more aware of your own mortality, an uncomfortable reality. You may face conflict with your siblings over an inheritance, or conflicting emotions if your relationship with your parent was strained or unresolved.

You may also be hurting for your *children*, who no longer have the unconditional love of a grandparent.

Perhaps you feel resentment that your *spouse* doesn't seem to get how much this loss hurts—or seems unwilling to help you care for the widow or widower who's now alone and needy.

As we articulate our understanding of how a loss has affected other family members, without evaluating or criticizing or ridiculing, we love each other well. Identifying our issues, feelings, and thinking patterns provides the foundation for addressing them.

HOW YOU'RE DOING

The answer to the question, "How are we doing as a family?" has less to do with how much hurt you're feeling and more to do with how well you're caring for each other.

Asking yourselves questions like these can help:
- How are we doing in listening to and validating each other's fears and concerns?
- How well are we doing in comforting?
- How well are we doing in lovingly confronting unhealthy coping and harmful thinking?
- How well are we doing in not insisting everyone else grieve in the same way and on the same timetable?

So . . .

How are you doing as a family?

You're hurting.

You're adjusting.

You're trying to find a new normal.

You're going through one of the hardest things a family ever has to go through.

So don't be in a hurry. Don't expect so much from yourself and each other. Give each other a lot of grace. Do everything you can to make your family a safe place to address your grief rather than avoid it.

And rest in the confidence that God is doing His part in bringing your family to a place of healing and wholeness. "He who began a good work in you will carry it on to completion" (Philippians 1:6).

God Fills In the Gaps

Q&A with Angela Robbins

*After Angela's husband, Wes, died of a heart attack while play-
ing softball with his family in the front yard on Father's Day,
his absence left a huge hole—a gap she thought could never be
filled.*

**In those early days after Wes died, what were your great-
est fears and challenges?**

I wondered, *Am I up to the task of raising my kids on
my own? How will my kids make it without a dad? How can
I go on? How will I live after this terrible thing? Will we ever
experience joy again?* It all looked impossible.

I remember when we were about three months into
being without Wes, we got in the car after church to go
eat lunch. The kids were arguing and I was in complete
despair. We were in such chaos. I pulled over on the side
of the road and got out and slammed the door and stood
in front of the car and said to God, "What were You
thinking? Do you see our life? How is any good going to
come of this? I don't get it."

After a while I got back in the car and told the kids,
"I'm really struggling without Dad. Sometimes I'm going to
get angry with God because I still don't understand and I
don't know if I ever will. But I know two things—He's big
enough for my anger and I know He is going to take care of
us. I know that no matter how bad it gets, we're going to be
okay."

What was that first year like for you?

The first year was all about just getting through all the
firsts—the first kids' birthdays without their dad, the first

Christmas, the first anniversary without Wes. We didn't do any of it very well. We stayed out of town in a hotel that first Christmas because being at the house without Wes was too painful. We did birthdays different. We tried to celebrate—but there was always the gut feeling . . . *It is never going to be the same. It will never be as much as it could have been if Wes was still here.* He was the one who brought the fun element to everything.

All family events were hard. Going to church was hard. Sporting events for my kids were so difficult. Any time you go out in public you feel like you have a neon sign over your head that says, THE FAMILY WITHOUT A DAD, THE BROKEN FAMILY. You feel like the spotlight is on you and that you look pitiful.

But as hard as the first year was, the second year was probably my hardest year. At that point, the reality set in: This is how it's going to be from now on.

I realized I depended on Wes so much for every part of my life and for so much of my identity. I remember bringing that up to my counselor, asking, "When am I going to be just Angela Robbins?" My counselor told me it would take my brain at least three years to change over into thinking of myself as just one person and not as half of a couple and it was absolutely true. I wore my wedding ring for almost three years. I wasn't ready to take it off. It made me feel like I was still married, and that felt good. It felt safe.

When did things begin to get better?

The turnaround for me began when I finally decided I would meet with another widow. I thought nobody could be in a worse situation than me. But once I sat down with another widow and she told me what she and her kids were going through, I realized I wasn't the only one with a difficult life. That brought me comfort. I introduced my kids to this family because I wanted them to see that they were not the only ones experiencing what it is like to lose a dad.

I thought I was dependent on the Lord before I lost Wes, but I didn't have a clue. Once I was stripped of the security blanket of my husband, I realized that I had never really learned what it means to depend on the Lord.

For a while I couldn't read my Bible, but then the Lord opened up the Scripture to me, and it came alive to me like never before. I began to seek an intimate relationship with the Lord like never before. I got to a place where I felt really clean before Him and was able to share things with Him that I never had before, like, "I'm lonely. I'm weary. There are times when I can't see the horizon and I need You to help me."

In what way did the Scripture come alive to you?

Honestly, at first I hated that verse, "He will be a father to the fatherless and a husband to the husbandless." I told Him I didn't like it: "I don't want that verse to apply to me." I didn't want Him to be my husband or a father to my children. I wanted Wes to be my husband and a father to my children. But that really was the answer.

So I began to pray, "Okay, Lord, You said You'd be the husband to the husbandless. I'm asking You to be that to me tonight. I'm asking You to fill every empty place in me. You know what that is. In Your own supernatural way would You minister to me tonight and equip me with the strength to get up in the morning and be what I need to be?"

There were scriptures I took as, *This is what I'm going to live on.* Like, "You are my rock and shield. I trust in

You." I would walk up and down the hallway in my house and say those psalms out loud, saying to God, "You are everything we need."

My kids began to pick up on it, and the tone around my home began to change. My kids began to see and celebrate how God was taking care of us. We'd be driving around trying to find a parking place and one would open up, and we'd say, "Jesus must have done that for us!"

One time in Target I needed something on the top shelf that I couldn't reach, and I thought, *This is so my life, here we go again. If I had a husband he could get that.* Just then another customer asked if he could help me. I realized immediately that God had filled the gap.

When you have so many gaps, they're real noticeable when He fills them. Even the tiniest detail means so much. He has done that so many times. It became so evident to us. We'd say, "That is so cool what God did!" It was someone being kind to us, but we saw it as God filling in the gaps.

In what ways would you say God has used the loss of Wes for good in your life?

So many ways. I remember one Sunday morning about two years into our journey, we were standing in church singing an old, great hymn. Worship songs have such a new meaning when you lose someone who is dear to you.

At that point, the Lord was just beginning to show us that He could fill our hearts. Worship was becoming a whole new avenue to express that for us. We were standing there singing and we wanted to shout. We couldn't sing the words loud enough or with enough passion. And my 12-year-old daughter said, "Look around. Nobody is feeling it like us. We're so lucky that it means this much."

What a blessing to realize you have a connection with Jesus you've never had before—because you've been able to share in His sufferings.

How do you deal with your kids' need for a dad and your own loneliness?

It is hard because you get a lot of pressure from your friends to pursue a new relationship with a man. To them, that is the fix to all your struggles.

But I've seen so many widows rush into another relationship and give up the opportunity to nurture an intimate relationship with Jesus. I tell new widows, "Do your best to pursue Jesus. Give yourself time to allow Him to fill every place. If you become a workaholic or shopaholic or go from relationship to relationship, you are filling your life with everything but Him."

I also know that if there is going to be another person in my life, it isn't for just me but for four people—and that's a tall order to fill. I do believe that the Lord will raise up someone for me, but in His time, and I have to trust that. There have been many times in the last eight years—especially as my kids are teenagers—that I think, *Lord, when will You send them a dad?* It's really more about them than me because I see how hard it is for them to go through those years without a significant male.

These are the times I go back to God and say, "I'm asking You once again to fill the gaps. I trust You with my life and with my kids' lives. I need to know You are actively involved in filling the gaps for my children."

What can you say today that you thought you'd never be able to say?

I can say that I really never dreamed that the Lord

wanted to bless us so much. I never dreamed He could create in us the capacity to have this much joy.

And I can say that if the Lord does not bring about another partner for me this side of heaven, I believe I still will have the most full life. I don't believe that at the end of my life I'll say I missed out.

I believe I've learned how to be content in whatever my situation because I've seen that He really can be enough. And not just enough, but way more than enough.

Chapter Two

When People Add to Your Pain

Nancy

The first thing I attempted to write after Hope died was an article I called, "The Worst Thing to Say to Someone Who's Grieving: Nothing."

Since then I've realized that nearly every person who goes through a significant loss emerges with a mission to put the world on notice about the stupid, hurtful things often said to those who are grieving—as well as the hurt caused by those who say nothing at all.

Certainly we heard our share of questionable statements. To me, the worst came from a man who told me God must have wanted one more angel in heaven. It was ridiculously sentimental in my book—completely unhelpful, just silly.

So I never expected to find *myself* wondering what to say to people who'd lost a loved one. Like most grieving people I've known, I determined that I'd never again say anything stupid to people in pain. But I quickly discovered that it's incredibly difficult to know what to say when you want to say something helpful and meaningful.

Two months after Hope died, David and I found ourselves attending two funerals in one day—one for a baby who had died at birth, and the other for a child who, like Hope and Gabriel, had Zell-weger Syndrome. As I was waiting in line to greet the parents at the first funeral, it hit me: *I have no idea what to say.*

Of all people, I should know what to say to these friends, I thought. But I didn't. There was no great wisdom that would answer the questions, no soothing truth that would take away the hurt.

I stumbled through both encounters and walked away with sympathy for all the people who, over the previous months, had struggled to know what to say to David and me. And I went away with more compassion for those who'd felt so helpless that they'd said nothing at all.

PUTTING OURSELVES IN THEIR SHOES

Have you noticed that when you go through a difficult illness or accident or lose a loved one, many people want to tell you a story about someone else who went through something similar?

We have a friend who was diagnosed with breast cancer. In the days following the dreadful diagnosis, many were anxious to tell her of people they'd known who'd faced the disease. There was just one problem: Many of the women in the stories died, and the storytellers were excited to tell her how happy the victims' husbands were with their new wives! It was really . . . not helpful!

David and I have a theory about this. We've decided that when people hear about difficulty in your life, their brains search like computers for a connection. Because they don't know what else to say, and in an effort to fill the awkward silence, they tend to blurt out the first "search result" that comes up: "I knew a family who had this happen . . ."

It makes people feel better to suggest a resource, a solution, a book—or to tell you about someone who overcame the obstacle you face. But it doesn't always make us feel better, does it?

To many of us, it feels like a subtle effort to diminish our loss—saying, in effect, that since the same or worse has happened to someone else, it shouldn't hurt us so much. I'm not sure why, but people tend to compare pain. *This is harder than that; that would be worse than this.* But you can't really compare pain. It all just hurts.

The truth is that most people are hoping to be helpful, trying to let us know they can relate in some small way to what we're going through. If we put ourselves in their shoes, we realize it's tough to know what to say to someone who's grieving.

We can be prickly and sensitive about the things people say to us that we wish they hadn't. Or we can choose to see their brains searching for a connection, their hearts wanting to show us they care—even though they may not have the words to express it well.

Giving Them Grace

As painful as it can be to hear someone say something hurtful, I think it's more hurtful when someone we know well chooses not to say anything at all about our loss.

I'm embarrassed to tell you that I kept very close tabs on people in our walk with Hope. I didn't make an actual list, mind you. But I knew who'd spoken to us and who hadn't, who'd called and who hadn't, who'd reached out and who'd withdrawn. My expectations of those around us were high, and I was often disappointed.

By the time Gabriel came, I'd learned that some people are gifted and called by God to bring grace to hurting people in the hard places; some people aren't. Some people are good in the note-writing department; some aren't. Some have the courage to pick up the phone; some don't.

Throughout our experience with Gabe, I was free from the tyranny of expecting so much from so many. I was free from the tiresome task of keeping a scorecard on everyone around me, taking note of who'd made an effort in our direction.

I've come to realize that much of what we label as uncaring is simply an inability to overcome the awkwardness, and fear of doing or saying the wrong thing. The reason some people have never said anything to you about the death of the one you love is that they simply don't know how to overcome the awkwardness. It doesn't mean they don't hurt with you or that they don't care. They just don't know what to say, and they fear that bringing it up will only bring you pain. They don't know how much you long to hear your loved one's name and some words of compassion—even if all they can say is, "I don't know what to say."

You can choose to be angry and resentful about that, building up a barrier in your relationship. Or you can choose to give people grace, accepting their inability to know the right thing to say or do.

Helping Others over the Hurdle

A few weeks after Hope died I was walking from one building at our church to another. My timing was bad. As I came out the door, four or five women emerged from the nursery building, walking toward me with babies in their arms.

I'm not sure who was more alarmed—the moms or me. I wanted to turn and run, to not have to face them or the awkwardness of the confrontation. But I also knew this was my chance to set these women at ease with me and my grief.

I'd figured out early that besides being the one to bear the grief, I also bore most of the responsibility for making things okay for the women around me who had babies. They felt awkward that they had children in their arms while mine were empty. It didn't seem fair to me that this was my job; but we've figured out by now that life isn't fair, right?

I realized that I could do what seemed natural: avoid these women and perhaps even resent them. Or I could step up to the plate and seek to overcome the hurdle of awkwardness with each one, setting us both free to enjoy each other.

That Sunday morning I stopped to greet the first woman I came to. As the other women filed by, I smiled and stroked the hair of the woman's daughter, Joy, born eight days before Hope. Then I went to my car and cried.

When you've lost a spouse or a parent or a child, everywhere you turn there are happy couples, attentive parents, and beautiful children. Even though you don't begrudge others the joy of these relationships, they're a reminder of what you've lost.

Let's face it: We're human, and it's hard.

So we have a choice. We can let everyone walk on eggshells around us. We can wait for people to do or say the right thing—as if there is a right thing. We can give in to our fear that things will never be normal with certain people again.

Or we can extend ourselves and do our part to set things on the pathway toward normalcy and wholeness.

LEAVING THE HURT BEHIND

When I speak and tell our story, I often open things up for questions at the end. When I did that recently, a woman whose mother had died stood up and asked how to handle her hurt and disappointment over the fact that everyone seemed to have forgotten her loss and moved on—while she was still hurting deeply.

The emcee of the event jumped in, encouraging the women of the church to remember to be there for those who'd experienced a loss. That's a great goal, of course, and part of our calling as the Body of Christ.

But I knew it wouldn't solve that woman's problem. The real

problem isn't what others do or don't do or say. The real problem is our attitude toward others who've hurt and disappointed us, and our unwillingness to let go of the offense.

If something doesn't shift inside us, we'll forever feel disappointed and hurt by the thoughtlessness and inattention of others. There has to be a breakthrough to find peace.

During Hope's life and in the months after she died, I often found myself churning inside. It seemed some of the people we thought would be there beside us in the midst of this trial had disappeared. At the lowest point of our lives, they chose not to enter in. They seemed to diminish our loss by ignoring it.

I was angry. But of course the anger was really a manifestation of hurt.

After repeatedly waking up in the middle of the night and rehearsing my put-you-in-your-place, here's-how-you-hurt-me confrontations, I wanted things to change. I knew resentment was beginning to take root in me; I wanted to be free of it, to let it go.

To do that, I knew I had to choose to release those who'd hurt me from the debt I felt they owed me. I knew I had to humbly ask the Lord to give me the spiritual strength to forgive them.

Taking it one step further, I had to start seeing my resentment as the real issue in my life—the sin I was responsible for. It was my resentment that was robbing me of joy, not what they had done or not done, said or not said.

I know you may be thinking, *Don't even think about suggesting that I forgive the person who hurt me.* You're sure he or she doesn't deserve it. The person probably hasn't even acknowledged what he or she did to hurt you. To forgive seems like saying that what happened doesn't really matter.

I understand. I've been there—or, I should say, I find myself there repeatedly, because no one goes through life without being hurt by other people. Sin takes its toll on all of us and our relationships. When we're already rubbed raw by the pain of loss, so many things and people rub us the wrong way, causing more pain.

But forgiveness isn't minimizing what someone has done, or saying that it doesn't matter. Real forgiveness is far more costly. It says, "You hurt me deeply, but I'm not going to make you pay. You don't owe me anymore—not even an apology." Forgiveness is choosing to absorb the pain and canceling the debt you are rightfully owed.

It is a choice. You can choose not to forgive. You can continue to play the waiting game with the person who hurt you—waiting for him or her to apologize, to make things right. If you do, you'll be allowing that person to hold you hostage. By saying, "If she apologizes . . ." "When he finally acknowledges . . ." "If they remember . . ." you depend on others to make the first move. And an unforgiving spirit weaves its way into the fabric of your entire life.

Or, you can choose to forgive. You can choose to abandon the agonizing animosity.

The Greek word for forgive, *aphiemi*, means literally "to abandon" or "to leave behind." Wouldn't it feel good to "leave behind" the burning resentment and the burdensome weight of hurt feelings?

Have you considered what impact your resentment is having on the rest of your family? Has it made you touchy and irritable? Has it interfered with your family's relationship to the person who has hurt you? Would other members of your family be relieved by your choice to forgive?

I don't think it happens instantly; at least it rarely has in my life. The deeper the hurt, the longer the process.

But that doesn't mean you can't start down that road today. You likely won't get rid of all your negative emotions immediately, but don't let that keep you where you are. Your first step toward finding freedom may simply be asking God to give you the "want-to." From there you take steps of obedience toward God and toward the one who has hurt you.

These can be costly, difficult, stumbling steps. But God will meet you at every one along the way, blessing you with the freedom that comes when you fully forgive.

What Kind of Grief Work Have You Done?

Q&A with Susan Shafer

The loss of her mother became the launching point of leading grief recovery groups in her church.

How did the loss of your mom affect your family?

The impact began while my mom was still alive, as I tried to balance caring for her through her battle with cancer and taking care of my two preschoolers. I felt pulled in both directions all the time. And then after she died I felt a constant pull between wanting and needing to sit in my grief and feel what I was feeling versus attending to whatever the emergency was with my kids.

At times I resented being a mom because I just wanted to be a grieving daughter. As I look back now, I realize that had I not had that demand on me, I would have easily sunk down into a pit. My children's need for me is what kept me afloat.

The night of my mom's funeral I can vividly remember panicking and saying to my husband, "I'm just afraid you are never going to get it," feeling that if he didn't get it, I would be completely alone. He had lost his dad two years prior to cancer, so he had an inkling of what I was going through. But his experience just wasn't the same as mine. He never did completely get how I felt.

But he didn't give up on me. I wasn't very rational, and was very demanding. But he didn't overreact; he didn't run screaming. He had a sense deep down that it would get better and that I wouldn't always be that crazy.

There came a critical time when my mom had been

dead for two years and I was clearly not getting any better. I was, in many ways, doing worse. I felt very alone and wasn't dealing with my grief in any constructive way. He finally said lovingly, "I am stepping up to the plate and insisting you get help. You can't go on like this."

I had played at talking to counselors and participating in a hospice grief group, but had never really made a commitment to work through the process of help that I needed. So I went to a Christian psychiatrist who really helped me work through the issues that I needed to deal with to find some peace.

Since then, you've regularly led grief groups that meet at your church and include people going through all types of loss. What have you learned in the process?

Everybody grieves differently. It is interesting to have a room full of people who are grieving and hear how differently they approach the grave, the way they choose to memorialize, how intensely they feel feelings, how differently they express them, the difference in the level of privacy they have about their loss. No one can ever assume that someone is going to respond in an expected way. You can't put your own issues, thoughts, and feelings about grief on someone else. It is too complex to do that.

I've also learned how important it is for grieving people to find an outlet—a person, place, or group—someone they can consistently and safely talk to about what is on their heart. You need someone you can say things to like, "I feel guilty . . . I feel afraid . . . I feel lonely," and then do it consistently over a period of time. If you don't release it that way it will come out in a quirky—and most likely unhealthy—way.

What are some of the common mistakes you see grieving people make?

The most common thing I see is people putting a deadline on their grief. We can get so impatient with ourselves, wanting it to be better so we won't have to feel this bad. Many people think, "I'll go through this eight-week grief group, and then I'll be done with this. I'll get my diploma and go back to life the way it was." They expect to be able to put it on a timeline and be done with it.

The reality is that the intensity of grief lessens but it never ends. It will always be a part of who you are—though not necessarily in your face like the first year or two. There is no formula and no time frame.

But I would add that while some people make the mistake of putting a deadline on their grief, others make the mistake of thinking that they are always going to feel as bad as they do now—which leads to despair.

Something I see especially in men who have lost a spouse is that they move too quickly into another relationship. They want to do whatever is necessary to put a wall between themselves and the unbearable pain they are feeling. They think, "My wife is gone, and there is a void in my gut. I don't want to feel that void. The only way to make that pain go away is to put someone else in there."

Some widows and widowers might say that they had time to grieve during their husband's or wife's long illness and therefore don't need time to grieve. And there may be some validity to that. But there is a huge difference between living with a sick person and the finality of death.

I've seen many men who have never had any one-on-one or group counseling after losing their wives. They don't want to talk about their feelings because it is painful. And then, in their very real loneliness they become convinced that filling the huge void with someone else will be the solution. Then, years later they find they cannot ignore the grief any longer and become desperately sad, finally grieving the loss of their wives. Unfortunately, they sometimes don't get to this place until after they've married someone else—and they struggle with resentment toward the new wife for her inability to fill up the empty place inside.

When I see someone getting into a romantic relationship the first year to two after the death of a spouse without having worked through their grief, it is a huge red flag. Widows and widowers always need to explore, "Have I really allowed myself to work through this?"

My first question to someone in this situation is, "What kind of grief work have you done?" And if they say, "Grief work?" it is a sign they have some work to do before entering into a new romance. There's nothing wrong with going on a date and enjoying someone's companionship, but moving too quickly toward intimacy and marriage can be a huge mistake.

What are the traits you've seen in people who are able to successfully work through their grief?

Good grievers find healthy outlets for their grief such as journaling, praying, talking to someone they trust, memorializing the person they've lost, acknowledging significant days, making a donation or doing a project in that person's memory. The goal is to find healthy outlets that aren't just busying oneself to cover over the pain but helping to vent the pain.

Communication is key—for the grieving person to be talking to someone on a regular, ongoing basis about the loss and feelings associated with it, rather than refusing to talk about the pain.

Healthy grievers recognize that God is comfortable with our grief. God doesn't judge our amount of faith based on how happy or sad we are on a particular day. If anyone understands grief, God does, and longs to be our Comforter. We can be gut-level honest with God. He can take it. He knows.

What are the benefits of being in a grief group?

Many churches and counselors offer grief groups that are built around the solid truths of Scripture and the hope found in the gospel. I recommend that the person grieving ask a lot of questions, finding out who the leader/facilitator is and what the format of the time will be. Do you have to talk? Are there going to be different types of losses represented? Do you follow a curriculum? Watch a video?

And I tell them, "You have nothing to lose by trying." You can always leave and never come back. But there is always the chance it could become the place you find the comfort you've been looking for in your desire for someone to understand how you feel.

I often hear people who attend a grief group say things like, "Just to be in a room with other people who are grieving makes me feel normal. Now I don't feel so crazy." There is no safer place than to be with other people who are going through the same thing you are going through.

There is so much power in saying things out loud. It provides a natural cleansing of the soul. It is huge. So many people start their sentences in the grief group with, "I've never said this out loud . . ." Once they say it, it doesn't sound so crazy and they find the other people can all relate to it.

Nobody goes into a grief group thinking, "I'm going into this group to give." But it happens, and it is oftentimes the first glimpse of the gifts God has given to a person in their loss. They find that there can be something good that comes out of it even if it is that they say one thing that helps someone else know they are not alone.

Chapter Three

Soothing the Hurt

Nancy

"Now I understand why people take drugs," I said to David the day after Hope's memorial service and burial.

I honestly had never understood it, because I'd never felt that much pain before. But now the pain was consuming, and I was willing to do just about anything to keep from feeling it.

So on that Sunday afternoon I went to bed, hoping to sleep the pain away. But when I woke up it was still there.

I remember wishing some friends might offer us their vacation cottage so we could make our escape. Yet somehow I knew the sadness would go there with us.

Work sounded like a good diversion, too. But I knew busyness would only put off the inevitable.

So would a movie. I would leave the hurt behind for two hours at the theater, only to have reality hit me between the eyes as we walked to the car.

When we're grieving and feeling desperate for relief from the pain, we look for comfort just about anywhere we can find it. We try to sleep it away, eat it away, drink it away, shop it away, travel it away, or busy it away. But it's still there.

We turn too quickly to the computer screen or the bottle or the refrigerator or the mall. So many of these favorite methods of self-medication not only fail to alleviate the pain; they add to it.

What can we do when the hurt is deep and inescapable and

we're tempted to soothe it in unhealthy or simply ineffective ways? We can turn from self-medication to self-ministry. We can learn how to comfort ourselves with the presence and promises of God, which are solid and sure and good.

Telling Yourself the Truth

When we're hurting, many people want to fix us and make everything better. Unasked-for advice is often free-flowing. Well-meaning friends and family tell us what we should do and how we should feel. They try to explain God's purposes and methods, which usually only adds to our confusion.

Then there's the voice inside our minds. Oh, the painful thoughts that go through our heads and make us wince!

I will never be able to be happy again.

My life is over.

I will be alone forever.

God must not love me.

God must be punishing me.

These desperate thoughts shape our feelings and assault our hope. The only way to find relief from these half-truths and outright lies is to learn how to tell ourselves the truth.

What are you telling yourself about your loved one's death, your current circumstances, your future, and what's ahead for your children? Is it true—thoroughly true? Can you differentiate between how you feel and what is true?

How we think determines how we feel. Our feelings are shaped by what we tell ourselves. So changing how we think and what we tell ourselves can change how we feel. Here are some examples.

- We challenge *I will never be able to be happy again* with the truth: *I feel very sad right now, but the time will come when I will smile and laugh again.*

- When we find ourselves thinking, *God must not love me,* we tell ourselves the truth: *I am deeply loved by God, even in the midst of this incredible loss. When I doubt that, I need only look at Jesus on the cross.*
- When our hearts are breaking because we think, *My children will never recover from this,* we remind ourselves of this truth: *God will provide everything I and my children need, and will use this loss for good in all of our lives.*

Some of the lies we tell ourselves have a shred of truth in them, which makes them easier to justify and hold on to. For instance, we tell ourselves, *Now that I'm no longer part of a couple, I will never enjoy our couple friends again.* The truth is that being with other couples may be awkward for a while, but not forever. Believe it or not, as you extend yourself to others you'll develop new friendships with people who enjoy you for who you are now—not as half of a couple.

While the reality of your loss can't change, what you tell yourself about that reality can change your feelings dramatically. We're not doomed to embrace the thoughts that run through our minds when we're distraught. We can argue with those thoughts and come to clarity and truth.

Our greatest source of truth to combat confusion and lies is the Word of God. But when I suggest that, I'm not talking about denying real feelings by quoting clichés and misapplied promises from random scriptures. I resent it when someone seems to pat me on the head with a Bible verse in a way that devalues my hurt and dismisses my deep questions.

I'm talking about confronting our very real fears, feelings, and thoughts with scriptural truth. I'm talking about digging deep in God's Word to figure out who He is and what His purposes are in the world and in our lives.

Truth soothes our fears, changes our feelings, and shapes our thoughts. The truth is what we need most when the hurt is deep.

PRACTICING HIS PRESENCE

A month after Hope died, I left home for a business trip on my own—thinking it might relieve my grief a bit. But in the darkness of my hotel room, as I lay alone thinking through the events of the night Hope died, I desperately wanted someone to remember with me. I didn't want to be alone with the pain. I began working my way through phone numbers in my memory and on my cell phone, but no one answered—which made me feel even more alone.

I tried to do what I've done most of my life when I've felt lonely, what most people do. I reached out to find another person to make the loneliness go away. But that night I couldn't find anyone.

In the days and months that followed, I found that even the physical or emotional presence of friends and family didn't always have the power to relieve the deep loneliness that accompanied my grief. I wanted to experience the presence of God in my life in a way that I never had before.

Maybe you've read God's promise found more than once in Scripture: "I will never leave you nor forsake you." We want to believe it's true; more than that, we want to *feel* it's true. But sometimes in our grief God can feel so far away. How can we begin to experience His presence in a way that soothes our pain?

"Even though I walk through the valley of the shadow of death, I will fear no evil, for you are with me" (Psalm 23:4). If we were honest, perhaps we'd have to admit that when we read that, part of us thinks, *Well, thanks. I was hoping for more than that.*

We simply don't value God's presence with us in this dark place. We want Him to show up and *do* something—give us the answer to our urgent prayer, provide instant relief from the ache of loss. But to just *be with us*? Is that all there is?

Truly experiencing the felt presence of God, however, begins with yearning for His presence, valuing His presence, and being willing to wait for His presence.

Hearing God's Voice

What I wanted in the hotel room that lonely night was to hear the voice of someone who really knew me and knew the sad circumstances of my life. But who knows the depth of our sorrow better than God? No human voice can comfort like the voice of God speaking into our sorrow.

And He does—through His Word.

"But," you might say, "I've tried reading my Bible, and it doesn't make sense to me," or, "It's so dry;" or, "It doesn't answer my questions."

I would ask, "Are you listening only for what you want to hear, or opening yourself up to what God has to say?"

We do this sometimes with human friends, tuning out what we don't want to hear and searching out those who say only what we want to hear. But when we're really open, we create time and space for listening. We lean in, think through each word, and wait patiently for the morsels that meet our deep needs.

It's the same with listening for God to speak to us. When we truly want His comfort and companionship, we set aside time rather than rush through it. We persevere in listening, chewing on words and ideas, opening ourselves up to be changed.

Sometimes He speaks comfort and assures us of His sovereign care in our lives. Sometimes He speaks conviction and points out patterns that need to change. Sometimes He speaks correction and clears up our misunderstandings of who He is and what He is doing.

When we open God's Word with a spirit of quiet humility and expectation, the Holy Spirit meets us and enlivens the words on the page. He applies those words to our hurting hearts, letting us know He has not left us to work through this loss on our own.

But a one-sided conversation doesn't soothe our pain. While we want to listen, we also want to be heard. We want to pour out our hearts to someone who cares, someone who will come alongside us and be touched by our sadness.

This is our privilege in prayer. Yet many of us see prayer only as our chance to present God with His to-do list for the day rather than as an ongoing conversation with a cherished friend.

What a relief it is when we can pour out our sorrows to God, laying before Him all our questions and needs and concerns. What a joy it is to begin a conversation with God, saying, "Lord, I want to talk to You about . . ."

This kind of deep, ongoing sharing makes us feel close to other people. And it's through this kind of sharing that we feel and know the friendship of God.

My friend Angela told me, "It took me two years after Wes died before I was willing to say to Jesus, in the coldness and loneliness of my bed, 'Jesus, I need You to make Your presence known to me.' " She admits it's awkward at times to speak out loud to God in the quietness of her room or to wait in silence for Him to make His presence known.

This is an awkwardness many of us have never been able to overcome. We haven't been quiet enough or patient enough to allow God to meet us. Perhaps we haven't really believed that being alone with Jesus will be intimate, intense, or invigorating enough.

God's very presence is His greatest gift to us. When we discipline ourselves to practice His presence, we discover for ourselves that it is enough to soothe and satisfy.

REACHING OUT TO SOMEONE ELSE

The week after Hope died, I was sitting on the couch reading a book by a man who had lost a child. He wrote, "There's only one thing I've found that helps with the pain."

You would have thought I was in the desert and he was telling me where to find water! I wanted to skip ahead. I wanted to know: *What is it that will soothe this enormous ache inside me?*

Then I read it: "Serving others."

Honestly, I felt disappointed. *That's it?* I thought.

Part of me said he was just a preacher who was giving me the party line. But I also thought that someone who'd hurt as he had wouldn't lie to me about where to find comfort. So even though I didn't really believe him, I decided to put what he said to the test. I was desperate.

Angela, widowed for less than a year, had just moved into a house in our neighborhood. The house had been empty for a while. The landscaping was badly in need of attention, and I knew she was overwhelmed.

So we loaded up our lawn tools and went to her house. We pulled weeds and trimmed hedges—and wept, for ourselves and for her.

As I exerted energy in serving someone else—and more significantly, as I thought about what it was like for Angela to leave the home she'd lived in with her husband, to set up a new home without him—my focus moved from my pain to hers. It was a relief, a distraction, an outlet. It was a reminder that I was not the only person in the world who was hurting. It was a step toward healing.

That day I discovered it was true: A secret to finding relief for your own pain is serving others in theirs.

Some people have told me they simply can't start reaching out to other people until their load of grief lightens. But I think reaching out in the midst of your pain—*because* of your pain—is the key to your unbearable load becoming lighter.

I've talked to women who've experienced a miscarriage who are comforted as they find they're uniquely equipped to listen to another woman who has miscarried and share her sorrow. I've known widows who find meaning in their loss as they provide companionship to those who've just lost their husbands. I've seen parents honor the lives of children who've died as they love other children their child's age—or other parents who've lost a child and wonder how they will get through it.

Second Corinthians 1:4 says that God "comforts us in all our troubles, so that we can comfort those in any trouble with the comfort we ourselves have received from God." Reading that, we may wonder if we have any comfort to share. But as we step out to serve others who are hurting, we discover God fulfilling His purposes in and through us—and our pain begins to lessen.

Will a Pill Help?
Q&A with Richard C. Shelton, M.D.

Richard C. Shelton, M.D., the James G. Blakemore research professor and vice-chair for research for the department of psychiatry at Vanderbilt Medical School, brings his expertise to the question of whether to take medication to assist with the grief process.

How does a person evaluate whether or not he or she should take medication to help with intense grief following the death of a loved one?

It is a hard decision to make. Feeling really sad is an appropriate, normal response to loss. And feeling really sad can also be part of depression. Sometimes it's very difficult to tell the difference.

Feeling really sad, tired, emotional, having trouble concentrating—these are symptoms consistent with normal grief. The more significant the death is, the more acute those symptoms will be.

In normal grief we would expect to see gradual improvement over time as the grief becomes less of a preoccupation. Within a few months the person with normal grief is sleeping and eating normally even though he or she may still be very sad. Talking to a grief counselor, a psychologist, a good friend, a Stephen minister, or a pastor are effective ways to work through this grief.

But this is very different from depression. When people are not only sad, but have sleep disturbances, appetite disturbances, low energy, fatigue, hopelessness, helplessness, suicidal thoughts—then we're seeing the signs of a physical illness called depression.

We know there is a problem when people go from thoughts of wanting to be with the person who died . . . to talking about how they might join that person in death; when they have lost more than 7 percent of their body weight within four weeks; or when they don't really feel sad anymore but are numb or emotionless.

These physical symptoms—along with negative thinking associated with being depressed—indicate treatment is needed. When someone's day-to-day life is significantly impacted with no signs of improvement over time—they're not able to go back to work, not able to do anything around the house—they should be evaluated for depression. And where there is any question, I would always err on the side of treatment.

Are certain people more prone to have this physical problem in the midst of grief?

People who have had a significant bout of depression before their loss are at very high risk for deep depression, and I would go ahead and treat them.

Many people are hesitant to take medication as we hear a lot in the media about side effects of antidepressants—such as suicide. Should a person be slow to take an antidepressant even when it is prescribed by a doctor?

There are limited circumstances where people will have an adverse reaction to medicine. There has been a lot of confusion about self-injury and suicide from antidepressant medications [Cymbalta (duloxetine), Zoloft (sertraline), and Lexapro (escitalopram) to Prozac (fluoxetine), Paxil (paroxetine), and Celexa (citalopram)]. And certainly there are people on occasion who take antidepressants and feel much worse rather than better in the short term. But this rarely occurs.

I suppose the question is, "Is it worth the risk?" Risk never happens in isolation; the risk of adverse reaction must be balanced against the potential benefit of treatment as well as the very real risks involved in no treatment.

Research shows that shortly after a loss, the likelihood that someone who is significantly depressed will kill himself or herself is significantly increased. But for the person with suicidal thoughts due to depression, going on antidepressants reduces that risk substantially.

Some people hesitate not out of fear of side effects, but because they have the sense that "God and I should be able to get through this." What would you say to that person?

I would say that they are applying a rule they would never apply in other situations. For example, if they have a dead battery in their car, they wouldn't say, "God and I will get through this," and keep trying to crank the car.

But people tend to apply a different set of rules or expectations for problems with their emotions or thinking or the functioning of the brain. They need to understand that with depression, the issue is chemical, not spiritual. There are chemicals in the body that are changed. The proper medication can normalize these chemicals so that people can function better, feel better, think more clearly.

Depression is caused not by a lack of spirituality but by abnormal physiology. A comparison to another common illness can be helpful here. An average person eats a candy bar, and the blood sugar surges up and then goes down again. But the person with diabetes eats a candy bar, and his blood sugar goes up and stays up.

Depression works the same way. Some of us have a physiological predisposition that makes it more difficult or impossible to rebound from the impact of grief like a person with normal physiology. So just like the diabetic needs insulin, the person with depression can benefit tremendously from antidepressants.

We know that there have been some incredibly godly people in history who have suffered tremendously with depression, and probably would have been grateful to have the medication we have available today—Martin Luther, Søren Kierkegaard, Charles Spurgeon. Their depression may have had nothing to do with their relationship with God or their spiritual strength, but everything to do with the level of chemistry in their brains.

So is medication the only way to deal with depression?

Frankly, for someone who is significantly depressed, most psychotherapy doesn't work. Research has shown that the main form of talking treatment that is effective for the depressed person is cognitive behavioral psychotherapy. I'm talking about by-the-book classic cognitive therapy, not just a counselor who uses cognitive therapy techniques. We use a workbook here called *Mind Over Mood: Change How You Feel by Changing the Way You Think* by Dennis Greenberger and Christine Padesky (The Guilford Press).

It is interesting, however, that 80 percent of people who are given the option of choosing between talking therapy and medication choose medication. Most people don't want therapy. They don't have time to come every week. And we see tremendous improvement in people who effectively use antidepressants.

Unfortunately, however, most people who take antidepressants don't take them correctly. Some take their medication sporadically rather than regularly, many stop taking it before they get past the short-term side effects, some aren't willing to escalate the dosage to an effective level, and some try to get off the medication too quickly.

If your doctor says, "I'd like for you to take an antidepressant for at least a period of time," I would suggest you give it a try for at least three months and ideally six months. It won't take your grief away; you'll still feel sad. But if you're depressed, it will keep you functional—and over time will relieve rather than simply mask your symptoms.

What is the difference between an antidepressant and an antianxiety drug, which some doctors recommend to patients going through the trauma of grief?

With antianxiety drugs [brand names would include Valium (diazepam), Librium (chlordiazepoxide), Serax (oxazepam), Tranxene (clorazepate), Xanax (alprazolam), Klonopin (clonazepam), and Ativan (lorazepam)] there is a difference between very short-term use and more long-term use in which a person takes the medication multiple times a day over a period of time. For acute, short-term use, where there are specific indications, and there are no depression indicators, antianxiety drugs are helpful.

For example, I have seen people who needed help to get through just the funeral or visitation. I have given prescriptions for an antianxiety medication and have found that it helps people get through those difficult events. Once the immediate situation is over, the medicine can be stopped.

Emotions have a quantitative element. Antianxiety medication brings down the intensity of emotions. It doesn't take the feelings of grief away, but it turns down the intensity.

But long-term use of antianxiety drugs is not the best idea for the person who is grieving. In addition to the reality that they produce dependency, they may also mask rather than treat depression symptoms.

Do you have to go to a psychiatrist to be treated with antidepressants?

Ideally that would be the case as psychiatrists tend to be more effective in monitoring the drug's effects and making needed dosage changes at regular intervals. However, primary care doctors write 80 percent of all antidepressant prescriptions. So if you suspect that you or someone in your family is not just experiencing normal grief but is, in reality, dealing with depression, start with your primary care doctor and don't put it off. Let your doctor help you determine if an antidepressant can help you.

Chapter Four

Keeping Your Faith in the Midst of Loss

Nancy

"Mom, is there any chance Hope might live?"

That was Matt's immediate question as he hopped into the car in the pick-up line after school.

I knew why he was asking. His second-grade class ended every school day in prayer. Naturally they were praying for Hope. And the only way they knew how to pray for Hope was to ask God to heal her.

So Matt needed to know: Should he expect God to do that or not?

"Well, God can do anything," I responded, not wanting to diminish the truth of God's power in his little heart and mind. "But I also know that no one has ever lived with Zellweger Syndrome, and that the doctors say we should expect to have her only a few months. What we do know for sure is that whether she is here with us or there with Him, she's in God's hands."

Prayer for healing. It's just "what we do" in the church, isn't it? Anything less can seem lacking in compassion, and certainly lacking in faith.

It was hard for me and David at times, knowing there were many who looked down on our faith because we didn't focus on crying out to heaven for God to heal our daughter—and, a couple of years later, our son. Some wanted to lay hands on our children and pray. They tended to look at me and say, "Well, I'm praying for a miracle!" They seemed to imply that if I was any kind of mother or Christian I would be doing the same.

In those hard days, David and I leaned heavily on the sovereignty of God. We grabbed hold of the hope that Hope would live exactly the number of days God intended for her, and that His purpose would be completely accomplished in that time. We didn't know what that purpose would be or how many days we would have, but we wanted it to be enough for us.

We sensed that faith would not be defined by throwing our energies into pleading with God to do things another way. It would be found in submitting to Him and saying to Him, "God, we trust You and we believe You are good—even though we don't believe You are going to heal our child."

Since you're reading this book, it's likely that you've lost someone you love. Unless that death was sudden, the last part of that person's life probably was marked by health issues. If so, did you pray for healing, for a miracle? Did someone hint that the strength of your faith would determine whether your loved one survived? Were there some who suggested you should recruit as many people as possible to pray, thereby elevating the chance that God would hear and respond to your request?

Now that death has robbed you of the one you love, are you wondering if things would have been different if you'd prayed differently or more faithfully? Has the whole thing made you cynical or skeptical or just confused about the role of prayer and faith in healing and death?

What does real faith look like in the face of death?

REAL FAITH, REAL HOPE

I suppose we begin answering that question by asking the more foundational one: What is faith? Hebrews 11:1 says, "Now faith is being sure of what we hope for and certain of what we do not see."

What do we hope for that we can't see?

In the rest of Hebrews 11 we read of people who hoped for a variety of things. But all of them hoped that the promises of God would become a reality—that God would provide a Savior who would bring salvation and redemption, making it possible to live with God in a "heavenly country" designed in God's mind and built with God's hands.

If real faith is placing our hope in Jesus' offer of salvation from the penalty of sin, and in an eternity in God's presence, how does that affect the way we deal with the pain of life in this broken world—including physical death? Accepting the death of someone we love calls for radically trusting God's plan. It calls for a faith that rests in God's sure purposes for suffering in this life—and His sure promises of the life to come.

Real faith was displayed by the psalmist who wrote, "My frame was not hidden from you when I was made in the secret place. When I was woven together in the depths of the earth, your eyes saw my unformed body. All the days ordained for me were written in your book before one of them came to be" (Psalm 139:15-16). This kind of faith believes that God perfectly planned the number of days He gave to your loved one, and that the number of days He gave was just right to accomplish His plan.

Real faith believes that "a good name is better than fine perfume, and the day of death better than the day of birth" (Ecclesiastes 7:1). On the day your loved one was born, he entered a pain-saturated, sin-scarred, darkness-loving, soul-depriving existence for a determined number of hours, days, or years. On the day of his death, if he'd placed his own faith in Christ, he entered a pain-free place of perfection that is ablaze with the glory of God, where his deepest longings are completely fulfilled—not for a number of years, but forever.

Real faith prays like Jesus, saying, "My Father, if it is not possible for this cup to be taken away unless I drink it, may your will be done" (Matthew 26:42). We freely tell our loving Father what we want. But because we know His plans are perfect and His way is best, we want what He wants—more than we want what our limited hearts and minds tell us we must have to be happy.

Real faith has the passion of Paul, who wrote, "For to me, to live is Christ and to die is gain. . . . I *desire* to depart and be with Christ, which is better *by far*" (Philippians 1:21, 23, emphasis added). By faith, we believe there is something better than physical healing and a longer life on this earth. It is leaving this life behind so that we might be with the One we love most of all—Jesus.

Being with Him won't simply be better than life here, but better *by far*. So we don't consider it a lack of love on God's part, or a failure of faith on ours, when He takes one of His own to be with Him. We just feel sad that we are not there with Him yet.

Real faith also rests in the character of God, especially when we face painful uncertainty over a loved one's eternal destiny. We remember God's description of Himself to Moses as "the LORD, the LORD, the compassionate and gracious God, slow to anger, abounding in love and faithfulness" (Exodus 34:6). We agree with the psalmist who wrote about God, "You are good, and what you do is good" (Psalm 119:68). We open our eyes to view the wideness of God's mercy.

When we're not sure about our loved one's relationship with Christ, we don't give in to despair. We rest in our certainty that we can trust God to do what is right with us, and with those we love.

How Much Faith Is Enough?

When I met Diane years ago, she was bright and energetic. But her wig gave away the all-out battle she was fighting against breast cancer. We asked God to work a miracle in her life and in her body, to restore her to health.

In her desperation, Diane drew close to a group of people who encouraged her to surround herself only with people who believed she was going to be healed. She began to turn away from many of us who wanted to walk with her on this difficult road. If you didn't believe absolutely that she was going to be healed, you were not welcome.

I suppose I understand where some of this comes from. I think of the paralyzed man who was lowered on a mat through a hole in the roof so that Jesus might heal him. Luke 5:20 says, "When Jesus saw their faith, he said, 'Friend, your sins are forgiven.'" The bold belief of this man's companions obviously moved Jesus. My friend, Diane, also wanted to surround herself with an atmosphere of faith.

But sometimes I wondered, *Faith in what? Faith in God, or faith in faith? Submission to God, or insisting on a particular outcome?*

Sometimes people seem to think they must prove to God that they have enough faith and no doubt—that God not only *can* but *will* heal them—before He will grant their request.

Does God really set up those kinds of hoops for us to jump through? How much faith is enough? How do you measure it?

In Luke 17:5-6 we read, "The apostles said to the Lord, 'Increase our faith!' He replied, 'If you have faith as small as a mustard seed, you can say to this mulberry tree, "Be uprooted and planted in the sea," and it will obey you.'"

Rather than giving the disciples a formula for increasing their faith, Jesus told them it isn't the *amount* of faith that matters, but its *object*. In fact, the *only* thing that matters about your faith is the person in whom you place it.

If the object of your faith is your ability to work up enough belief to impress God, your faith will be as weak as your will. If the object of your faith is a particular outcome for your situation, your faith will be as weak as your wisdom. But if the source and object of your faith is Almighty God—even if that belief is of the mustard-seed variety—your faith will be enough for whatever God allows into your life.

It's not your job to impress God with the amount of faith you can work up on your own. It's up to you to receive and live out the measure of faith God gives you.

Every ounce of your faith is a pure gift of grace from Him. He will give you the grace not only to accept the death of the one you love, but also to be faithful to Him as you grieve your loss.

This is what real faith is—a gift of God that enables you to keep loving and following Him even when His plan is not yours, even when death has taken away the one you love. God promises that His gift of grace will be enough.

THORNS AND GRACE

It had always seemed a bit like a pat on the head to me, the words spoken to Paul after he asked three times for his suffering—the "thorn in his flesh"—to be taken away. When I read the Lord's response in 2 Corinthians 12:9—"My grace is sufficient for you, for my power is made perfect in weakness"—it seemed He was brushing off Paul's earnest request, ignoring his pain, withholding the healing He had the power to give.

But that's before pain pierced my world, before I prayed my own desperate prayers, before I found out that the grace God would provide would be exactly what I needed when I needed it. That's when I discovered that His grace would be enough for me, even if He didn't take away the pain.

Paul knew the purpose for and source of his pain. The purpose: "To keep me from becoming conceited because of these surpassingly great revelations" (vs. 7). Paul had been given a guided tour of heaven, a tour given to only a handful of faithful followers. Evidently God knew that such a magnificent experience could turn Paul into a braggart. So God supplied what Paul needed to keep him humble.

But Paul calls this thorn in the flesh a "messenger of Satan" (vs. 7). So which is it? Was this thorn from Satan or from God?

Perhaps if Job had been able to see the conversation behind the scenes of his life and loss he would have had the same question, don't you think? Maybe you've asked it about losing the one you love: *God, is it You who sent this pain into my life, or was this sent by Satan to hurt me? Who caused this, and why?*

Paul shows us that the sovereignty of God extends beyond our narrow categories for cause and effect. While Satan may have sent a messenger with the purpose of hurting Paul, God had decided to use that pain for His own good purpose.

This gives us hope that God will use the pain and loss in *our* lives for His own good purpose, too.

But what, you wonder, could possibly be a good purpose in your suffering?

God uses the physical pain that doesn't subside, the relational pain that puts us on edge, the pain of grief that brings us to tears, to get our attention and turn us toward Him. Pain brings us to our knees. We begin with prayers for our pain to be removed. And then, as God works in us, we begin to pray that the pain will be redeemed. God used the pain in Paul's life to move him from pleading for relief to taking pleasure in Christ's power being displayed through his suffering.

Rather than giving Paul the healing he asked for, God gave more of Himself, His grace, His strength. The fact that I once saw this as a pat on the head rather than God's generosity and sufficiency reveals my small thoughts of God, my trivialization of His grace, my underestimation of His strength.

Perhaps you can relate. When God offers us Himself in the midst of our pain, when we read His promise to be with us, most of us think, *That's it? That's the best You can do? I was hoping for more.*

The truth is, we're often more interested in getting what God's got—not getting more of God. We've put in our order for a miracle of healing, and the miracle of His presence seems like the consolation prize. But God knows exactly what we need, and His purposes are grander than giving us what we want. He's doing something deeper.

In the 199 days we spent with Hope, and during Gabe's short life, people would often say things like this to us: "I don't know how you are doing this. I could never do it."

Sometimes we would respond by saying, "You're right. You couldn't do it, because God has not given you the grace for it— because you don't need it, at least not right now. But know this: When you do need it, He will give you all of the grace you need."

I've learned—not only because God promises it in His Word, but because I have *experienced* it in the lowest places of my own life—that the grace God provides is all we need. It is enough for whatever we face.

You can rest in this promise: God's grace will be delivered to you in the form and quantity and timing your circumstances require.

The grace God provides is enough to generate joy in the midst of great sorrow. It's enough to help you endure the loneliness of your bed, the empty place at the table, and the reminders of loss everywhere you turn. It's enough to enable you to continue believing God is good and that He loves you.

This has been a very freeing discovery for me. Realizing that I may have many more years to live, recognizing the possibility of more difficulty and loss in my life, I have more confidence and less fear than I had before. I completely believe that whatever God allows into my life, He will also give me the grace to endure faithfully.

What the Lord said to Paul, He also says to you and me: *My grace is sufficient for you today and for everything you will face in the days to come. It will be enough for whatever I allow into your life.*

This promise is no mere pat on the head. It's our most prized hope as we face an uncertain future.

Seeing God's Goodness

Q&A with Gracia Burnham

Gracia Burnham and her husband, Martin, worked as New Tribes missionaries in the Philippines for 15 years. In May of 2001, they were taken hostage by the Abu Sayyaf, a militant group seeking an Islamic state, and spent a year as captives in the jungle. A rescue attempt by the Philippine military resulted in Martin's death. Gracia was released and returned to life in America as a single parent. You may want to read Gracia's incredible story in her book In the Presence of My Enemies *(Tyndale House).*

When you look back at that first year of life after Martin died, what would you say were your biggest challenges?

I went from being a really simple, unknown person to being thrust into the limelight, and I didn't know how to handle that. I thought for a while I was just getting my feet back on the ground, and then I would get to go back and do what I had always done and be who I was before. It took me three years to figure out that I can never go back to being a simple, obscure missionary overseas. This life is what God has for me now. This is the new normal.

Making sure my kids were okay was my biggest priority. Kids that are 15, 13, and 11 don't talk a whole lot. To keep the lines of communication open, I spent a lot of time in the car. I would take them places—even without a destination—just to be in the car, because that was when my kids would talk as we all faced the windshield. I made sure we did things together and didn't fall into the trap of just watching TV and not talking. I also volunteered a whole lot at their school. Some people saw that as a waste

of my time and energy with so many competing demands
for my time. But to me that was important, even if I was
just shelving library books. I was in the same building as
the kids, able to stay in close touch with them.

What has the grief process been like for you?

I did a lot of my grieving in the jungle. And when I
came home, I found myself full of joy and happy and trying to make the most of our new family God let us have.
To have each other, and for my kids to have their mother,
is a real gift.

To be honest, I'm not sure I really know what grief is.
If it is extreme sorrow, I have waves of that. Not wishing
things were different, just sorrow. But every time I feel
deep sorrow, at the same time I'm also so happy we are a
family. The goodness of God is so huge in our lives. Sometimes I almost feel guilty for being sad, because God has
been so good.

**How is it that you are able to see God's goodness rather
than focus only on your loss?**

For me it is everywhere. People have been so kind to
me. I have food that tastes good and the money to buy it, a
nice home, and people stopping by because they care
about me. When I go to the music programs at school, I
realize it is such a privilege to be there because I couldn't
be there when we were in the jungle—though Martin and
I would try to imagine it.

I listen to uplifting music, songs about God's goodness, and I have good books to read. I see the goodness of
God in having a Bible and sitting down anytime I want to
read it. And there is always a message appropriate for
today in there.

I went for a year having nothing. Just brushing your teeth was a wonderful thing to get to do. I know what it is like to not have things. And I'm very aware that I have more than so many people in the world. I think of the women who live in the Sudan who have experienced loss after loss after loss—their husbands have died, their kids have been dragged off into military militias—the loss those women live with makes mine look like nothing. And it helps me to be grateful for what I have.

In America we are so used to having everything. I'm not making light of a loss in America, but if we can see how much we do have, and rejoice in the children getting us out of bed in the morning, or in still having a husband after we've lost a child to help us go through it, the sense of gratitude will lead us to contentment.

For me, the key has been my mind-set. I was suddenly showered with good things and to be ungrateful would have been flagrant sin. Maybe that is why the kids are doing well. I've just told them over and over that we have so much to be thankful for.

How are the kids doing?

I'm not sure I ever saw what most people would define as signs of grief in my kids. And honestly, that bothered me. It still bothers me today because I want to make sure the grief does not affect them in negative ways as they move through life.

While I had done a lot of my grieving in the jungle, I think my kids grieved a lot during that time, too. My son's grades went down, he had detentions at school, and was always in the counselor's office. To them, they had effectively lost their parents. I remember when Jeff was being interviewed by a reporter and was asked, "What is it like not having a dad now?" And he said, "Well, we thought both our mom and dad would die in the jungle. So when our mom came home, we decided to be really happy we have a mom, and not be upset that we don't have a dad."

So I never saw them grieve a lot for Martin. We talk about him and laugh about crazy things he always did. In fact, last night my 16-year-old and I were driving to Block-buster to return a movie, and my son said, "Dad would have said, 'They don't make movies like that anymore.'" And I said, "I really miss that guy." And he said, "I do, too."

My son told me recently that when he meets a man he is impressed with, he looks for the qualities that are like his dad. He likes to say that his dad is in heaven scouting out the cool places to show him when he gets there. We talk openly about how good it is to know that we will all be together one day in heaven because we all know and love the Lord.

Chapter Five

Heaven Matters

Nancy

I didn't give much thought to heaven before Hope died.

I believed in it, but I didn't think about it much. And I certainly didn't long for it.

For most of us, our focus is here on earth—on what we can see and touch and know. But that changes when we lose someone we love, doesn't it?

Suddenly heaven matters. A lot.

But some of us get a little annoyed at those around us who seem to think heaven is the easy answer to our pain.

"She's in a better place," someone says.

And we think, *But I want her to be here with me.*

"You will see him again," someone else says, trying to offer comfort.

And we wonder, *But how long will I have to wait?*

I remember going out on our back patio on a dark July night, a few weeks after Hope died. Through tears I looked up at the stars and vented my thoughts about Hope: "I know you're in heaven. But heaven feels so far away from me."

The truth is, confidence in heaven doesn't solve the problem of grief. But as the promise of heaven sinks in, it can salve the hurt.

Heaven isn't a superficial, sentimental coping mechanism for facing death. It's our sure hope and solid joy. The more we search for what's true about heaven and apply it, rejecting the fantasies, the more its promise brings rest to our grieving hearts.

WE CAN ONLY IMAGINE

A couple of months after Gabe died, a music industry friend called and asked David, Matt, and me to be in a music video. A band that was unknown at the time—Mercy Me—had recorded a song that was starting to get significant radio airplay, and a video was being created to play behind the band's performance of the song at the upcoming Dove Awards.

The producers invited a number of people who'd lost loved ones to come to an old house where the video would be shot. Each person was asked to bring a picture of the loved one. So David and Matt and I brought our two large portraits of Hope and Gabe and somberly looked into the camera to do our part.

The song was "I Can Only Imagine." We'd heard it just a time or two, not realizing it would become a huge hit—and a huge blessing to many people.

I can only imagine what it will be like, when I walk by Your side . . .
I can only imagine what my eyes will see, when Your face is before me!
I can only imagine. I can only imagine.

Surrounded by Your glory, what will my heart feel?
Will I dance for you, Jesus? Or in awe of You, be still?
Will I stand in Your presence, or to my knees will I fall?
Will I sing "Hallelujah!"? Will I be able to speak at all?
I can only imagine! I can only imagine!

I can only imagine, when that day comes, when I find myself standing
*   in the Son!*

I can only imagine, when all I will do, is forever, forever worship You!
I can only imagine! I can only imagine![1]

It was fun to be a part of the video, and I love the song. But the video has always represented to me our conflicted thoughts and feelings about heaven. While the words celebrate the joy and focus of heaven being the presence of Jesus, the visual images hint that our longing for heaven is perhaps more about seeing those we love who've gone before us.

During Hope's life I was sent a book called *A Grief Unveiled* by Gregory Floyd. And in the quiet of the week after she died, I finally sat down to read it. I found myself underlining phrases and sentences that echoed my own pain and questions.

The book was written by a man of deep faith who lost a son. At one point the author quoted his wife, Maureen, who said, "I really want to go to heaven to see Johnny, but I'm struck that I want to go almost more to see him than to see Jesus."

I could relate to that, and maybe you can, too. Suddenly I found myself longing for heaven. It seemed so real. Yet, if I was honest, it was not Jesus I was longing to see and enjoy most of all; it was Hope.

It seemed a sad commentary on the inferior state of my love for Christ.

To be honest, though, I think this longing reflects our inescapable humanity. Right now we know and love Jesus through a glass, dimly, and we long for the day when we'll know Him face-to-face. But when we lose a child or spouse or parent, it's someone we've seen with our eyes and touched with our hands and loved up close.

I think God understands this intense longing we have to see and enjoy the ones we love. He made us to love each other deeply.

I also think this longing, in the hands of God, is a tool He can use to awaken us to Himself. It's one of the most significant ways He uses for good what we may see as bad. When someone we love is in heaven, it becomes more real; our yearning for heaven becomes more vivid. And to long for heaven is a gift of grace.

People we love are precious to us, and our reunions with them in heaven will be grand. But the fact that we long for them more than we long for Jesus reflects our limited understanding of the beauty and magnificence of Jesus. In heaven, we will see Him in His fullness; we won't have to choose between focusing on the people we love and loving Jesus with our whole heart.

In heaven we'll have perfected bodies, perfected thoughts, perfected affections. Our celebrations and songs will be about the Lord. When that day comes, we and our loved ones who know Him will look together to Jesus.

A BETTER PLACE BY FAR

Many people find a great deal of comfort picturing a loved one in heaven, imagining what he or she might be doing and enjoying. Personally, I haven't done much of that. Heaven seems so impossible to imagine, I don't know where to start. Since I don't know how to draw that mental picture, I'm uncomfortable to find my imaginings on the subject fueled more by movies and paintings than by Scripture.

I give little credence to books by people who claim to have seen heaven and come back to tell about it—and there are plenty of them. But there are a few exceptions—in the Bible.

I believe what Isaiah wrote about his view of heaven in Isaiah 6. I trust what John recorded in Revelation about the guided tour he was given. And I have confidence in what Paul writes about his experience of heaven.

Paul's experience especially intrigues me. Explaining in 2 Corinthians 12 that he was "caught up to the third heaven" (vs. 2), he adds, "Whether it was in the body or out of the body I do not know—God knows. And I know that this man . . . was caught up to paradise. He heard inexpressible things, things that man is not permitted to tell" (vss. 2-4).

Not permitted to tell? I can't help but feel disappointed when I read this, because I'd like to know! Wouldn't you?

At least I know Paul is a person I can trust when he tells me about heaven. One of the best things he tells us comes earlier in that letter to the Corinthians—something simple but profound that can inform our own perspective: "We are confident, I say, and would prefer to be away from the body and at home with the Lord" (2 Corinthians 5:8).

He would rather be absent from his body. Having experienced both heaven and earth, he chooses heaven. He said much the same in Philippians 1:21, 23: "For to me, to live is Christ and to die is gain. . . . I desire to depart and be with Christ, which is better by far." Obviously Paul didn't see heaven as a modest improvement on life in this world, but *far* better.

Sometimes we give lip service to the idea that heaven will be better. But we live as if heaven is second prize—and staying here longer is the goal, the better option.

That's one reason why, when someone we love dies, we see it as a tragedy. We get so caught up in how that death hurts us, we find it hard to truly celebrate when that person is ushered into God's presence.

This reality came home to me when Hope was a couple of weeks old. We were in the balcony at our church's Christmas program. Sitting there with Hope in my arms, I began to mourn all the things I would never get to enjoy with her. As I watched the children's choir sing, I mourned that I would never get to see her do that. I began to think about all the other things I would never enjoy with her—a gourmet meal, a new dress, a first kiss, a good report card, a great vacation.

The tears began to drip down my face onto Hope. I was starting to let go of the dreams I'd had for sharing with her the good things of this world. It felt like a tragedy.

But then it hit me. My perspective was oriented to earth. And she was headed to heaven. I realized that the best earth has to offer is only a taste of the perfection of paradise.

Over the weeks that followed, I began to consider other earthly things Hope would "miss out on." There would be no allergies or acne, fighting weight gain or feeling left out, broken dreams or broken hearts. She would leave a world marked by crime and cruelty, disease and disappointment—and enter one of wholeness, richness, perfect beauty, and peace.

This change in perspective made a difference. It didn't take away my sorrow over losing my daughter. But letting the truth of what was ahead for her simmer in my mind had an impact on my feelings. It helped me let her go.

When David was interviewed about the night Gabe died, he said, "While it was one of the most excruciating moments of my life, it also was not hard to envision that he took his last breath here, and took his next breath in the presence of God."

I love that thought. That is the promise of heaven: To be absent from the body is to be present with the Lord.

That's worth waiting for—even longing for.

The Long Goodbye of a Long-term Illness

Q&A with Max Lucado

The losing began for bestselling author Max Lucado long before his parents died.

Your dad was diagnosed with ALS [Amyotrophic Lateral Sclerosis, or Lou Gehrig's disease] shortly before you left the states for missionary work in Brazil. What was it like to take in that diagnosis?

I had just taken my first ministry position in Miami, Florida, and was preparing with Denalyn to go to Brazil when Dad was diagnosed. I wrote him a long letter, questioning whether or not I should move ahead with my plans to go. He wrote me back a letter that I have framed and hanging in my office today. He told me that he had no fear of death or eternity and that I should go to Brazil and fulfill the call God had placed on my life. It was a gift that he gave me his blessing to go.

He was in his late sixties when he was diagnosed and in stable health, but was disabled within a matter of months after the diagnosis. About a year into the disease he was put on a ventilator, which meant he could no longer talk, and the last year he was unable to get out of bed. I made several trips back to see him during my time in Brazil and was with him when he passed away.

More recently you experienced the death of your mom after a long illness.

My mother, who died last May, moved to San Antonio six years ago so we could look after her as she suffered from dementia and needed significant care. Eventually we moved her into a nursing facility and I tried to see her most days, but some days all I could do was call to check on her. Those years were marked by a cycle of guilt and frustration over managing her world as she was completely dependent on us for care.

In the end, it was a blessing to have time with her, to know her. And it was a good learning experience for our daughters to be around a person in her nineties and to see what it is to grow old.

As you and your family have experienced the long-term illnesses followed by the death of your parents, what have you found helpful?

When a family member dies, it is not just a slight change in how that family operates. It really rocks the boat. A voice you are accustomed to hearing, an opinion you've come to rely upon, is now silent. This kind of change begets fear before it does faith. There is a sense of panic. To me, coping with the death of a family member means coping with the fear of what this huge change is going to mean, and how you will continue when your world is so different.

I've found it helpful in my life, in times of major transition and change, to purposefully remember what has *not* changed. It's helpful to make a list. God's love, His available intimacy, His sovereign plan—these things about God have not changed. And likely many other things have not changed—perhaps you still live in the same house, still have other family members. Purposefully accounting what has not changed helps to offset the transition required by what has changed. I call that digging deeper and holding on.

How did the loss of your parents affect your faith?

My mom's death was expected. She lived a healthy life till she was 86 and died at 91, having enjoyed a lot of good years.

My dad had finally retired and he had aspirations of traveling and camping and enjoying life with my mom. So we felt blindsided by his disease and perceived it as tragic.

For me personally, I felt disappointed in God. I thought He would heal Dad on this earth and He didn't. I had not had many occasions in my life with crises of faith, but that was a significant one for me. At the end of the day I decided to trust God, but it took me awhile to get there.

What are the unique aspects of grieving the loss of someone who dies after a long-term illness?

In a long-term illness, the one you love dies a little more every day. So at the point of death there can be a surprising lack of sadness because you've said goodbye over weeks, months, or years. There comes a turning point when we're watching someone die that we catch ourselves thinking, *They need to go. It would be better for them.* It comes with prayer, tears, and heartache. But because you see their suffering, you finally say, "Lord, take him."

The person who loses a family member under those circumstances faces the cemetery completely different from the person whose loved one is taken suddenly. For them, the grieving is just beginning.

I've had conversations with families who have lost a loved one after a long illness and they felt guilty they weren't grieving. They felt happy the person they love didn't have to suffer any more. And I could relate. I try to help them see that they are not experiencing a lack of grief, but an abundance of grief. They've been grieving for two or three years. "The fact that you are not over-whelmed is a sense of unselfishness," I encourage them. "The fact that you are happy is a statement of faith."

Oftentimes, in an extended illness, the person we mar-ried, or the one who raised us, or the child we bore—we haven't seen that person for a long while. They've been bedridden or not able to communicate or not themselves anymore at all. We may not have known it, but we were burying a little of them every day. The letting go of grief has been a gradual process.

Have you seen any good come out of the losses of your parents?

Seeing the courage with which my dad died showed me how to die in faith. His death is part of our family story. It brought me and my three siblings together and unified us after we had dispersed to separate lives.

Dad planted a tree over the grave where he would be buried, and whenever we go home we stand by that tree. It's become a symbol for our whole family.

The truth is, we don't need to feel the pressure to be able to point to what we would describe as the "good" coming out of our losses right now. The odds are that someday we will see those things. But we don't have to see it now to be confident that it's true.

Chapter Six

Staying Together

Nancy

I've heard it over and over—and you probably have, too.

I'm talking about the claim that 70 to 80 percent of couples who experience the loss of a child end up getting divorced.

It's a scary statistic. It can add to your fears about how grief might affect your marriage.

But according to a 1999 survey, and affirmed in a 2006 survey conducted by Compassionate Friends—a support organization for parents who have lost children—this statistic is simply a myth. In the more recent study, only 16 percent of couples who had lost a child got divorced.[1] That's far below the divorce rate of 40 to 50 percent of average U.S. couples married for the first time.[2] The reality is that the death of a child appears to draw more bereaved parents together than it pulls apart.

You're not destined to divorce if you face the grief of losing a child. In fact, the sorrow you experience together may actually bond you in a way you weren't connected before.

Still, losing a loved one can strain a marriage—adding to the pain and building walls that isolate spouses when they need each other most.

ONE GRIEF, TWO PATHS

Because of the common perception that losing a child can spell the end of a marriage, David and I are often asked what our "secret" is.

People see that our losses have driven us closer rather than tearing us apart, and they want to know why.

I wish I had a secret—something surprising and solid and universal that would salve the deep hurt and bridge the divide that grief can cause in a marriage.

I certainly don't have any simple answers or surefire formulas. If I did, you'd instinctively know they were unreliable and probably inapplicable to your unique relationship and issues.

But I will share with you a few things that have helped us along the way.

When Hope was born, we spent a week at Baptist Hospital in Nashville. She was undergoing a battery of tests to confirm or rule out the Zellweger diagnosis. We were being trained to feed her with a tube and take care of her other needs.

But I really think they kept us there for a week out of kindness. We were a couple in extreme shock.

Since we were sharing Hope's difficult diagnosis with only a few very close friends, the stress was bundled up inside us. As we did our best to put on a good face for visitors and reckon with the realities of continuing bad reports from test results, three very special nurses cared for Hope—and for us.

One of them brought me a book. And what a pivotal gift it was.

A Mother's Grief Observed by Rebecca Faber (Tyndale House Publishers, 1997) was a book of reflections from a mom whose child had drowned. I read it voraciously, thinking, *This is what is ahead for me.*

I came to a chapter where the author described the toll grief was taking on her marriage. She resented that her husband didn't seem as sad as she was, and that he'd gone back to work. He seemed just to be moving on, and a chasm was developing between them.

But then she discovered that every day on the way to work he was pulling to the side of the road to weep for a while. She realized it wasn't that he didn't grieve, but that his grief was taking its own form and its own time. And it was not something he felt comfortable releasing with her.

I read that chapter out loud to David in our hospital room. "We'll have to remember this," I said. "It might be this way for us, too."

So even as Hope's life began, long before the intense grief following her death set in, we were preparing. We were starting to understand that our grief would likely take different paths, and that those paths could lead us apart if we let them.

A Bridge Too Far?

I've often likened the effect of grief on a marriage to a train going over a wooden bridge. If the structure was fractured to begin with, the weight and trauma of the train will probably cause it to collapse. Even if the bridge is strong, the train's crossing will reveal areas of weakness that need to be shored up. It will expose cracks beneath the surface.

This is one reason I'm uncomfortable answering the question about how our marriage survived. We'd been given the gift of a strong marriage before grief "ran over" us. It wasn't perfect—not free of difficult issues or disappointment in one another. But it was good, intimate, fun, solid.

I've often wondered what would have happened if Matt, our firstborn, had been born with Zellweger Syndrome. We were younger, married only three years, more self-centered; our faith was defined more by our church responsibilities than by a growing relationship with Jesus. I don't know what the death of our firstborn would have done to us.

So while I have no "three easy ways" to hold a marriage together in the midst of unbearable sorrow, I'll share with you what seemed to help us.

1. *Talking.* David and I are talkers. No, we're communicators. As much as we were able to put our awkward feelings and creeping fears into words to each other, we did.

But even more helpful was all the talking we did with others. We worked through our thoughts and feelings and theology and questions as we described what we were going through. We talked across the table, over the phone, and sitting around the living room with many, many people. Talking helped to release the pain and relieve some of the fear.

After a devastating loss, it's common to go home and hide. But we welcomed the world in. I suppose it was a bit intimidating for many of these people; they weren't sure what to say or do, and wondered if they were imposing on our privacy. But the process of talking about what we were going through—not just medical details but the spiritual questions, emotional issues, relational challenges—helped to bond David and me together in our convictions and concerns. Each of us learned what the other was thinking and feeling not only by saying it to each other, but in overhearing it shared with someone else.

When there are no words spoken about your loss, assumptions are made and walls are built. Talking keeps you on the same page as a couple. Hurt comes when we assume what our spouse is thinking and feeling, but intimacy comes as we talk about it.

2. *Touching.* There is so much about grief for which there are no words—only a desperate, awkward loneliness.

For a married couple, nothing salves that deep loneliness like meaningful intimacy. But with meaningful sexual intimacy comes pleasure. And pleasure is a very uncomfortable experience in the midst of grief.

To feel pleasure, to give yourself to the sexual experience, letting go for a few moments the intense sorrow in your soul, seems—at least for a woman—a bit like betrayal. It creates a real inner conflict of the heart, mind, and body. You wonder, *How can I allow myself to feel so good in the midst of feeling so bad and so sad?*

Yet it's such a welcome release of the pent-up emotion and the desperate loneliness. What a comfort sexual intimacy can be in the midst of deep sorrow. It requires a lot of patience and tenderness, and perhaps even an allowance for tears. But it offers a closeness that helps to forge a strengthening against the battle grief wages against a marriage.

3. *Expecting.* Reading that book while still in the hospital room helped prepare us to grieve differently from each other. I didn't expect David to fix things or take care of everything or express emotions in a certain way. He didn't seem to expect me to get happy, get over it, or even get up in the morning.

Proper expectations—or perhaps very few at all—helped to keep us from the disappointment and potential resentment that come from unmet expectations.

David gave me the gift of allowing me to grieve in my own way and my own timing. I gave him that gift in return. Our deep confidence in each other and in each other's love for Hope and Gabriel allowed us to give each other space and freedom and grace.

4. *Praying.* Early on David and I found ourselves often praying together in our bed in the dark. They were weak and simple prayers, unimpressive, inconsistent.

As time went on, we began to pray less often. We felt guilty, knowing that so many people were praying for us.

Still, we were unified in our ongoing conversations with our Father. We struggled through what was appropriate to expect of God. We wrangled with the various perspectives coming at us about healing and heaven, God's sovereignty and God's sufficiency. This spiritual unity was a solidifying force.

If you've never had the habit of praying together, it may feel awkward to initiate. You may stumble through it at first. But now is the time to begin to pour out your hearts to God together.

5. *Sharing.* Perhaps the most bonding aspect of our experience was the shared passion and sense of mission that emerged from it.

Death has a way of changing the conversation with everyone; we found we had very few meaningless conversations during our season of sorrow. Instead of talking about our lawns with our neighbors, we found ourselves talking about life and death and faith.

The emerging ministry that came from sharing our sorrow with the people around us became a shared purpose. It bound us together in beautiful and fruitful ways.

We've observed couples who have not emerged from loss with a shared mission; one or the other may have the passion to make a difference in the lives of other people because of their loss, but not both. This adds to the strain on a relationship as the weeks and months pass, leaving each spouse feeling very alone.

Finding something to pour your joint energies into after you've given yourselves time to process your grief will help you grow closer—and add meaning to your suffering.

6. *Respecting.* A month after Hope died, we were at a restaurant with friends from another city who hadn't met our daughter and wanted to hear the whole story. As we poured it out over pasta and bread mixed with tears, David said something I'll never forget. I think it is the best and only true secret I have to offer in terms of staying together.

With one arm around me and the other hand pointing toward me, he told our friends, "You should have seen her. She was incredible."

It meant everything to me. It still does.

It helped us define an intangible yet very real reason we grew closer together rather than apart during our experience of loss. Seeing up close how we responded to incredible loss and disappointment, we grew in respect for one another.

You can't hide from your spouse what's really going on inside. As we walked through the days and nights together, facing frightening unknowns and painful realities, we grew in admiration for each other. I was amazed and impressed by David—by his solid faith and his ability to articulate it, by his tender strength, by his firm grasp of unbearable facts, by his courage and commitment.

The bottom line was that our up-close view caused us to grow in respect for one another. And that respect drew us together.

You can't control how your spouse responds to this loss. But you can control how you respond. Have you reacted so far in a way that would cause those closest to you to grow in admiration of your courage and faith?

It makes me desperately sad when I hear about a couple that loses a child and then a marriage. I can't imagine adding to the agony of losing a child the pain of losing the one person who most closely ties you to that child.

Grief forces a marriage into unfamiliar terrain that requires a new set of communication skills, a new level of unselfishness, and acceptance of a "new normal." The new territory can become a place of barrenness and dryness and ultimately death for your marriage. Or it can become fertile ground for your relationship and respect for each other to flourish.

My Perspective on the Secret of Staying Together

David

One might say the real "secret" to a marriage surviving, even thriving, through grief is to choose a good mate in the first place. That was certainly my secret!

Of course, when tragedy strikes your family, it's too late to make that decision. We are who we are, and our marriage is what it is.

Few of us have advance warning of catastrophe in order to "get our act together" and be sure our marriage is ready to weather any storm. Most of us are hurled into loss with all the warts, conflicts, and other baggage of a less-than-perfect marriage. We may feel like the relief pitcher thrown into the game in the eighth inning with his team behind by seven runs.

Marriage can be hard enough under "ideal" conditions. But when pain, shock, and grief are added to the equation, the challenge can seem insurmountable. No doubt this is why some partners throw in the towel along the road of grief. But I do have a "secret" to share that can help you and your family.

Our secret is *not* that we are exceptionally strong people. The mental picture I have of Nancy and me walking through grief is of two wounded people leaning on each other as we limped along. Neither of us felt equal to the task.

We had been told our daughter would die any day. We felt the crushing disappointment of knowing that she would not grow up, walk, go to college, marry, and have kids—or even see or hear us. We endured the awkwardness of acquaintances, doubts about having more children, and uncertainty about the effects of loss on our son and our parents.

In our shaken and weakened state, our strength faltered and our knees buckled. We leaned into each other. When two people do that, they can't help but get closer.

Sometimes this leaning was literal. Often Nancy, who is 10 inches shorter than I am, would bury her face in my chest and sob. These were difficult moments for me; I didn't know what to do or say.

Frequently these episodes came without warning—sometimes immediately after close and joyous moments. Often she would begin to shake uncontrollably, and finally the audible cries would pour out. I did the only thing I could: I held her tight. As it turns out, this is exactly what she needed.

Usually the leaning was emotional. Somehow, by God's grace, we looked out for each other that way, drawing strength from each other in our weak moments.

Those moments came often. We grew tired of answering the

same medical questions, of hearing stories from well-meaning people about "my friend's brother-in-law's cousin who had a sick child, and she turned out fine . . ." We became discouraged when our moments of trust in God were followed immediately by meltdowns over mundane events like coffee spills or lost car keys.

We never agreed overtly to bear each other up instead of finding fault in one another's emotional frailty. But, thank God, this somehow became our unspoken mode of operation.

As you face your own family's loss, I urge you to get on each other's team. Hold each other up. Look for opportunities to support each other and come to one another's emotional rescue. This is crunch time. It's not the hour to keep score of grievances or unmet expectations. It's time to support, defend, give grace, love, and pray.

Remember, though, that you can't do it all. As much as we drew strength from each other, that strength reached its limit. In our struggle we reached out to God, individually and as a couple, and He met us in our need.

We experienced His promise: "My grace is sufficient for you, for my power is made perfect in weakness" (2 Corinthians 12:9). We began to understand the reality of living one day at a time, because we often felt we'd been granted strength for just one day. Tomorrow we would go to Him for more.

I fear this oversimplified appeal—"Depend on God in your suffering, and He will help you"—will seem nothing more than a spiritual platitude. This is especially true if you're not only enduring great loss, but also seeing your marriage or family being torn at the seams. But I believe it is our only true hope.

Jesus says, "Come to me, all you who are weary and burdened, and I will give you rest" (Matthew 11:28). In Jesus, we have a Savior who understands our suffering, loves us completely, has prepared a glorious and eternal future for us, and has sent the Holy Spirit to be our Comforter and Guide as we struggle through this fallen world. As much as it can help to lean on each other in desperate times, our true strength and the true hope for our families is in Him.

What's the secret to staying together when tragedy and loss seem to be unraveling us from inside and out? It takes nothing less than the miraculous work of the Holy Spirit in our hearts, producing His fruit, rather than our own feeble results. It's what Paul calls the fruit of the Spirit. Take a look at the list in Galatians 5:22-23. What impact could attributes like love, joy, peace, patience, kindness, goodness, faithfulness, gentleness, and self-control have on your marriage as you deal with losing a loved one?

Experiencing suffering together offered us the surprising opportunity to see the fruit of the Spirit displayed in our lives, our marriage, and our family as never before. We found that when we reach the end of our own resources and lean into our loving God for strength, His Spirit can work in and through us to produce the fruit that pleases Him—and that gets us through our seemingly hopeless situation.

Chapter Seven

Her Grief

Nancy

I remember when it really hit me for the first time. It was a couple of days after receiving Hope's diagnosis. We left the hospital briefly to have Thanksgiving dinner with David's parents and Matt.

As I sat in the restaurant, panic began to rise inside me. I couldn't chat anymore. I just looked at David and said, "We have to go—*now.*"

While David pulled away from the parking lot, I began to let it out—a guttural cry bordering on a scream. It ripped out of me as I bent over in pain. The truth was beginning to sink in: My daughter was going to die, and I didn't know if I could bear it.

David was helpless to soothe me. What could he do to fix this? Nothing.

I'm sure it scared him. I'm sure it made him fear what this loss was going to do to his wife, who'd always been so happy and so much fun. Perhaps that day he began to wonder if he'd ever get his old wife back—or if she was gone forever, lost to sorrow.

Recently I went to lunch with a woman who was grieving the suicide of her adult son. She was beginning to feel the pressure that so many mourning women feel from their husbands—to accept it, get over it, move on, get things back to normal. But her world had been rocked and there was no moving on—at least not yet.

Men tend to get nervous pretty quickly when their wives are

desperately sad and don't seem to be snapping out of it. They begin to wonder, *Is she going to be like this forever? Is she ever going to get over this?*

In their desperation, these husbands often do two things that actually slow down the healing process rather than speeding it up.

First, they act as if they're unaffected by the sorrow—or at least only mildly affected and certainly have it under control. Perhaps they feel they must be the "strong one" of the family, or they simply experience and express deep sadness differently from the way their wives do.

I suspect most women who conclude that their husbands are doing fine while they're falling apart themselves feel abandoned. They think their husbands are unwilling to go to that deep place of pain with them, leaving the wives on their own.

The second thing some husbands do is to drop subtle, and not-so-subtle, hints that enough time and energy have been given to this sadness thing—and that it's time to feel better and act happier.

Husbands may do this because they're afraid their wives will stay this way forever. Perhaps some of it is selfish, but surely not all. The husband sees the woman he loves suffering deeply, and wants her to feel better. Yet he has nothing to pull out of his tool kit that will fix her.

He tries setting the pace by example, but she can't keep up. He tries reasoning with her, which makes her feel he just doesn't get it. He tries avoiding her, ignoring her sadness, which leaves her all alone.

So how can a husband *really* help?

After Hope died, I felt I had a choice. Here I was, a mass of pain—a big, red blob of burning hurt. I could choose to try to stuff that hurt into a closet to deal with later or ignore altogether. Or, I could bring the hurt into the open—expose it to the Light, tend to it, allow it to drain its potent poison so that I would slowly heal.

I knew leaving it out in the open would be messy for me and everyone around me. But it was the only way to shrink the hurt to a manageable size. I also knew that if I stuffed away the hurt, it would only become larger and less manageable and would ooze into my life at inopportune times and in unexpected, unhealthy ways.

If you're a husband and your wife is trying to work through the loss of a loved one, here are three things you can do.

1. *Give her time and space to release the pain.* Do you want your wife to stuff away the hurt so life can *seem* to get back to normal? Or do you want her to truly heal so that both of you can find a *new* normal? If the latter, you'll need to give her time.

How much time? It might take a *long* while. And even though this may not be what you want to hear, it might get worse before it gets better. You're going to have to be patient.

When you love someone, letting go is a painful process that takes time, and it need not be rushed. For your wife to lock away her pain is, to her, like saying the person she loved didn't matter.

In reality, your wife's tears are your friend. There is so much sadness inside her that *has to* come out; tears are the healthy way to release it. So don't rush her through them or see them as a sign that she's broken forever. They're the healing balm her heart desperately needs.

2. *Make a place in your life together for this brokenness.* The grief books I read during and after Hope's time with us advised me not to expect a return to life as "normal," but to create and accept a "new normal." Frankly, I had a hard time understanding what that meant. Maybe I still do.

I don't think it means accepting that you'll always feel as badly as you do when the loss is fresh. Yes, there will be a place inside you that hurts forever. But that doesn't mean you have to hurt *the way you do now* forever. Nor does the hurt have to remain the focus of your thoughts and energy and emotion.

For now, rather than ignoring the hurt, you make it a group project—with the goal and determination that your family eventually will be released from the tight grip of intense grief.

Perhaps creating a new normal means you recognize that your loss has changed you as individuals and therefore as a family. It's altered your perspective and priorities. It's changed the makeup of your family, and you fit together differently now.

Rather than resenting or ignoring the change, you make a place for it in your life and in your family identity. You accept that there is a broken place inside each of you that will always hurt a little. But it doesn't mean that hurt will always be at the forefront of your minds or control your emotions or cast a shadow over every event. For a while it will—but not forever.

3. *Ask how she wants you to respond to her tears.* I figured out pretty quickly that David just could not win. I had so many tears that needed to come out—and no matter how he responded, it seemed to be the wrong thing.

Lying in bed, I would begin to weep. If he moved to comfort me, I would halt my heaving and sobbing. I knew it hurt him to hear and feel the evidence of my pain, so I did my best to rein it in even when I wanted to let it out. But if he stayed on his side of the bed and ignored my tears and sniffles, I felt hurt that he seemed to be disregarding my pain.

Once I figured out that David was in an unwinnable position, I realized that I needed to release him from my high expectations. I couldn't assume he knew how to soothe or respond to my erratic, grief-induced expressions. I needed to gently tell or show him if there was something he could do. You may need to ask your wife to tell you what you can do that will help and not hurt.

So will you ever "get your old wife back"? Not exactly. But it's likely that, as you give her the time and space she needs to grieve, she'll feel better and smile again. She'll get that sparkle in her eye once more and throw her head back in laughter.

While this loss may change her, it may deepen and refine her. It may even transform her in such beautiful ways and bond you to her so strongly that you wouldn't take your old wife back if she were still here.

A WORD TO WIVES:
HELPING YOUR HUSBAND HELP YOU

While husbands have a unique opportunity to love their wives well when the latter are crushed by sorrow, we can't expect our husbands and children to read our minds or know exactly what we want and need. We have to do our part of dealing with grief in healthy, constructive ways—so that we can be the wives and mothers we truly want to be.

Here are four things you, as a woman who is grieving, can do to lessen the impact of your grief on family members—and help them know how to help you.

1. *Make time and space to release your pain where and when it won't add to your husband's and family's pain.* I've shed a lot of tears while driving in my car by myself. That's when I had time to stop and think, and inevitably tears would come. I'd have to "suck it up" when I got where I was going.

I've wept as I walked in the park near our home. The year after Hope died, I cried on airplanes a lot. Eventually I stopped putting on makeup before my flights, so I could get a window seat, turn my head toward the window, and let the feelings out, drowned out by the noise of the jet engines.

But I also needed a place in my house where I could go when I felt the tears bubbling up—a place where David and Matt didn't have to see or hear me, where I wouldn't cast a shadow of sorrow over the entire house. So I would go up to Hope's room, close the door, lie on the bed, and let it out.

Is there a place you can go and a time you can go there to get your tears out, a place where your husband and family won't have to hear every sound or see every sign of your sadness? They love you. Seeing or hearing your deep sorrow can hurt them and leave them feeling helpless.

2. *Tell your husband and children what you want and expect in those awkward, tear-filled times.* The grief counselor we saw after Hope died told Matt that when his mom was crying and he just ignored it, it was like there was a skunk in the middle of the living room and nobody was talking about it. She suggested some words to use in those moments, like, "Mom, I see you're sad and I'm sorry about that."

We have pretty high expectations of those around us when we're grieving, thinking they should know how to act, how to help, what to say. But no one can crawl inside your head to know what you're thinking, inside your heart to know how you feel, or inside your will to know what you want. You have to reveal these.

You can gently guide your husband and other family members by affirming when they do or say something right—or when they try. Sometimes you may have to be more direct: "I know it must be hard for you to know how to act or what to say when I'm really sad. A quick hug or squeeze of my hand lets me know you recognize that I'm having a hard time and that you care."

3. *Expect to be lonely in your grief; don't assume your husband can take the loneliness away.* When you boil it down, the essence of grief is intense loneliness. No matter what your husband does or doesn't do, even if he responds perfectly to your pain, you will still feel desperately lonely.

In our hurt we may look around and think, *If I'm this lonely, it must be because my husband isn't there for me in the way I need.* But when we realize that intense loneliness is the essence of grief, we stop expecting that our husbands should be able to salve that sore spot. We stop taking out the frustration of loneliness on the person closest to us.

4. *Let your husband know that your goal is healing, not to stay forever in this painful place.* Some husbands fear that if they give their wives permission to be sad and stay that way, they'll be condemning themselves to a life sentence of being around a terminally sad woman.

What a drag—really. Put yourself in your husband's shoes. Ask yourself how much fun you are to live with and how hard it must be to please you these days.

You can give your husband a gift of hope. Let him know you appreciate his willingness to give you time and space to release your pain through tears and sadness. Tell him you look forward to the day when the sadness will not dominate your thoughts and emotions. Let him know that you believe the day will come when it won't hurt so much anymore—and that your sadness *now* will actually help to usher in that day.

Chapter Eight

His Grief

David

We've heard it many times, and know it's true: Men and women typically process life differently.

So it shouldn't come as a surprise that we handle grief differently. Every individual is unique in his or her experience of grief, regardless of gender. But because men and women typically display different characteristics when dealing with grief, it's helpful to understand and accept that a man might not respond to loss as the women in his life do.

In their book *Men Are Like Waffles, Women Are Like Spaghetti* (Harvest House, 2007), Bill and Pam Farrell point out how we men generally need to compartmentalize our lives—like the little squares on the surface of a waffle—to make sense of and get a grip on the various facets of our existence. We have the work box, the marriage box, the father box, the recreation box, and on and on. We tend to focus on one box at a time.

By contrast, the Farrells propose that women's lives are like a plate of spaghetti. Rather than being confined in individual compartments, the roles and responsibilities and relationships and thoughts and feelings are strands intertwined and intimately related to each other. These strands not only connect the elements of their lives, but the connections contribute importantly to the woman's sense of being accepted and belonging.

This means, among other things, that only women are truly able to multi-task. Nancy and I can leave the house at the same time in separate cars and return 90 minutes later, having driven an identical number of miles. When we compare notes, it becomes painfully evident that while she did the grocery shopping, picked up the dry cleaning, took lunch to a friend, went to the post office, made a deposit at the bank, and executed an important conference call, all I managed to accomplish was to go to Home Depot and buy lightbulbs!

Maybe this speaks more to her giftedness and my general ineptitude, but I think it illustrates a common reality. Women are typically skilled at integrating the diverse elements of life, and men are typically gifted with focusing on one thing to the exclusion of others.

When grief hits, many of the differences in how we process life come into play. We rarely see it coming, and may not be prepared for our contrasting responses.

For men, there isn't a waffle box big enough to contain the loss of a loved one. We'd like to be able to go into that compartment, take care of it, and emerge in good enough shape to handle our other challenges and responsibilities. Try as we might, however, we're brought to the uneasy realization that grief just doesn't work that way. It seeps into every area of our lives. This makes us uncomfortable, disoriented, and fearful.

If you're a wife, consider the following responses many men tend to have when a family loses a loved one. Understanding that these reactions are normal, and expecting them in your household can help make them less intimidating for you and less threatening to your relationship.

1. *Silence*. Why is he keeping everything bottled up inside? Why isn't he talking to you about his feelings? Is he feeling anything at all?

There are probably several reasons for the troubling silence.

First, he is processing it all. He likely hasn't been here before, and there is no instruction manual. He is gauging its impact on him, on you, on your friends and family. He's revisiting what he believes about God in light of the crushing blow of loss. He's testing his own feelings internally, having a healthy respect for their power lest he unleash them on those around him.

As a man, he may not be as practiced as you are in sorting out and articulating emotions. In fact, he probably doesn't see the practical benefit in doing so. He wants the pain to go away, not to keep coaxing it to the surface.

2. *Doing.* Why is he rushing back to work so soon? Why is he out trimming the shrubs . . . now, of all times? Why is he so energized to exact retribution on the doctors, or the driver of the other car?

Typically, a man deals with crisis by trying to figure out what to do. When death strikes, we come face-to-face with the problem we cannot solve, and it is tremendously unsettling.

After losing a loved one, many men appear positively manic in their rush to get busy, trying to regain their equilibrium. That's not easy in our culture, where most death-related work has been "subcontracted" to professionals. When a death occurred in earlier times, males in that family or community would go to work building a coffin, digging a grave, carrying out burial and funeral rituals, attending to effects and belongings, and providing food and transportation to survivors. In our society today, those tasks are assigned to funeral directors and cemeteries and preachers and others; men are left to stand awkwardly about in uncomfortable suits, feeling lost, helpless, and useless.

3. *Inactivity.* Why can't he seem to get moving again? Will he ever come out of this depression? Can't he see that he's stuck in his grief, and why won't he reach out for help?

There is a flip side to the "doing" coin. Some men dealing with the loss of a family member become immobilized, finding it nearly impossible to return to work, to carry on formerly meaningful relationships, even to get out of bed in the morning.

When we believe it's our job to solve all problems, and are steamrolled by the problem for which we have no solution, our despair can tempt us to throw in the towel. A man may fight valiantly beside the bed of the terminal patient, pursue the breakthrough treatment, or rally heroic prayer; but if death prevails and the battle is lost, there is simply no more fight in him. This can be a paralyzing condition, and much love and prayer and counseling may be needed to encourage the man who's lost his sense of purpose, meaning, and significance.

4. *Anger.* Why does he seem so mad all the time? Why all the talk of revenge? How can he think it's okay to take it out on you, especially when you're already in pain?

Grief is an emotion closely related to desire. When the desires we've had for our loved ones' well-being and for our relationship with them are ripped away, we grieve. And we get angry.

Men are particularly wired to think of themselves as defenders of their families. Usually we don't get the chance for a fair fight with the disease or the accident or the murder or the suicide. Even if there seems to be nobody but God to blame, we're still mad. This anger is often taken out on the most undeserving of victims—our co-workers, our families.

Ideally, the grieving man in your life has some healthy outlets for this very natural emotional runoff. Whether it's a punching bag in the garage or evil aliens on the video game screen, unbreakable targets for our grief-fueled anger are good to have around. Physical and mental exertion are important healers for men in grief.

Many wives are understandably distressed when their husbands display anger in any form. Too many women have suffered physical, verbal, or emotional abuse at the hands of angry men, and this is tragic. But just as you wouldn't want your man sanitized of healthy desire, righteous anger is a sign of life that desperately needs its proper outlet.

We need God's perspective on anger. He gets angry—at sin, at forces of wickedness that would steal not only our joy, but also our soul. Sharing God's passion for holy delight and His anger at sin and death can motivate men not to destroy, but to live lives of purpose and significance.

5. *Diversion.* Why is he talking about everything *but* the death of the one you love? Why does he change the subject whenever you bring it up? He seems to be pretending that nothing happened; how could he think you'd want to take a vacation this year, after your loss?

This is part of the "waffle way" of processing life. Your man is not necessarily insensitive or trying to avoid reality. He simply wants his life and your life to regain some sense of balance and comfort. He'd like to replace the pain with a little happiness, and is doing what seems natural to him.

Seeing himself as the protector, this ship's captain is steering you and your family away from the sad realities. He's instinctively trying to guide you toward things that have brought joy in the past, or would seem to offer normalcy or stability.

Unfortunately, he probably doesn't understand that diverting attention from the loss may be keeping you from getting your sadness out. Too much diversion can prevent you from remembering your loved one together and validating that person's place in your lives. Sharing these strong feelings as a couple is part of your love relationship.

HUSBANDS: HELPING YOUR WIFE UNDERSTAND YOUR GRIEF

If you're a man, do the previous descriptions sound familiar? Being a man myself, I'm pretty certain what your initial reactions are.

First, you size up whether you're normal. Good news: You probably are.

Second, due to years of cultural conditioning, you look for indications that you're a jerk. More great news: You're not a jerk. You're
a man.

Third, you read between the lines for clues about how your
responses to grief might affect the women and children in your life.
At least I hope you do.

What makes the challenge of getting your family through the
loss of a loved one so difficult is that you must do three things:

- Find a way to deal with your own grief.
- Stay aware of other family members' needs.
- Be sensitive to the impact your grief is having on the rest of
  the family.

In other words, traveling together through a great loss presents
you with the unavoidable opportunity to help your family through
the pain—or add to it.

You need not be Superman to be the helper you want to be. But
you'll find it easier if you keep in mind a few things your wife
longs for.

1. *Listen*. You may think your wife wants you to talk, but what
she really wants is for you to listen to her. She knows that requires
a conversation. If that isn't happening, it may be because you aren't
willing to pick up your side of this two-way interaction.

Don't worry; she'll do enough talking for both of you. I mean
this in the kindest, most respectful way. Women generally have more
words at their disposal than men do, and women tend to process
their feelings by verbalizing them. I'm sure it hasn't escaped your
notice that the proportion of female-to-male contributions to this
book illustrates that!

Your wife needs to talk out her feelings. She needs to know you
hear her. So don't be in a rush. Don't try to guide her to solutions

and answers and explanations. Be patient, listen, and be prepared for it to feel uncomfortable.

Because you love your wife, you don't want her to hurt. You want to fix the problem. But what needs to happen is for her to release her feelings by verbalizing them.

Amazingly, as you allow her to do this, you probably will discover some thoughts and feelings awakening inside you. Sharing some of those with her will be an incredible gift to her. It also will strengthen your relationship and become something you have in common as a couple.

2. *Stay close.* In the darkest times of her grief, Nancy seemed to curl up deep inside herself. Since she'd always been such an open person, this was strange and a bit frightening to me. Feeling insecure, I instinctively retreated from her as if I'd been rebuffed.

In bed at night she would often turn her back to me, curl into a tight ball, and cry. If I tried to comfort her, I felt her tense and disappear deeper like an armadillo inside its shell. I'm not sure I ever totally got over the feeling that she wanted to shut me out, that she was telling me, "There's absolutely nothing you can do to make me feel better, so don't even try."

Somehow, mercifully, I began to understand that this wasn't what was going on. I sensed her actions weren't a statement about how she felt about me. They simply demonstrated the crushing pain she felt over losing a child.

I told myself that she needed me, and that I had to avoid using these episodes as a barometer of my worth to her or her feelings for me. I determined in these moments to stay close, hold on to her, mostly keep my mouth shut, and just be there.

If you're experiencing some of these awkward and even disturbing times of coolness with a grieving wife, it might help to think about what she's experiencing as being like physical pain or injury. If she'd just broken her leg skiing, you wouldn't be surprised or offended by her lack of tender affection. You'd stay close, do what you could to help and look out for her, and tell her you love her.

3. *Be strong.* I don't mean John Wayne, or even Jack Bauer. I just mean this is the time to stand up and be a man.

What does that involve? Psalm 27:14 says, "Wait for the Lord; be strong and take heart and wait for the Lord."

Getting your family through the loss of a loved one is not a sprint. It is an endurance race.

We think of being tough as the ability to beat up the bad guys, take the best shots from the enemy, stand tall, and not be fazed by tragedy. But that's the Hollywood version of being strong.

Waiting for the Lord is tough. It takes courage. Your wife and family are not expecting you to be superhuman in the midst of this loss. They are not anticipating Braveheart. What they're looking for is your leadership in standing before God and saying, "I can't handle this. I can't fix it. God, I am looking to You for strength, and I will muster the courage to trust You to get us through this."

In the closing words of his first letter to the Corinthian believers, Paul urged them succinctly, "Be on your guard; stand firm in the faith; be men of courage; be strong" (1 Corinthians 16:13).

I like that. In your family's most difficult challenge, you have the opportunity to be the man.

Does that mean you put your wife—and children, if any—on your back and carry them safely to the other side? That sounds appealing, but it's utterly unrealistic. What you have is the opportunity, with God's help, to stand firm in your faith, take courage, and wait on the Lord.

Following 1 Corinthians 16:13, after the admonition to stand up and be a man, is this: "Do everything in love" (vs. 14). You demonstrate your love for your wife and family by remaining visibly committed to trusting God alone for their eternal stability and security.

As you already know, the loss of a family member is an unimaginably painful crisis you cannot fix. Only God is sufficient to meet us in that desperate place. But you have the critical and beautiful opportunity to be the one who keeps leading your family there.

Be a man, take courage, and wait for the Lord.

Grieving Alone Together:
Another Couple's Story
Q&A with Rex and Connie Kennemer

Rex and Connie Kennemer have been full-time missionaries with Church Resource Ministries for over 20 years. But everything in their world changed on November 17, 2005. That's when their son, Todd, a victim of bipolar disease, took his own life at the age of 25.

It has been just over a year since your son, Todd, lost his battle against mental illness. What has grief been like for you?

Connie: I've been surprised at how different our grief has been. Rex and I are close as a couple, and we loved Todd with the same depth. So we expected we would feel and process the same things the same way, but our experiences of grief have been radically different.

I didn't experience the profound grief Rex did immediately after Todd's death, though one might think as his mother I would. Honestly, it was embarrassing. We would be in a setting where we would be talking about Todd and Rex would break down, while I would respond with this strength. I wasn't faking it; I just had a reserve. But I also thought, *This can't be right. I should be the one sobbing instead of Rex.*

Rex: In the early months, I was a kind of vegetable. I didn't want to go out and do anything, and that was embarrassing. I also had the luxury of a three-month sabbatical, which Connie didn't have and most people don't have. I don't know how people go to the funeral and then go right back to work.

Connie: But that was how I coped. The fact that I led a

team of other people was my life-blood. I could submerge the huge sorrow I felt just by working, and knowing that there was purpose ahead. I have a hero mentality: *We'll fight this thing and make it better for someone else.* Work and this sense of purpose kept the huge sadness below the surface for me for a while.

Rex: Another way our grief has been different is that I was mad at God. I felt like He was the only one big enough to do something about Todd's illness, and He didn't.

Connie: I was mad at Todd—mad not only for what he was putting Rex and me through, but my whole family through. My parents are in their 80s. I could see that their pain was taking years off their life, and I thought, *Todd, what were you thinking?* That is when I would cry and scream, and then I'd be done and move on.

Rex: I started journaling and expressed a lot of my anger in my journal. About six months after Todd died, I had the opportunity to read parts of my very raw journal at a ministry conference—and I cried through it in front of 500-plus people. That was a turning point for me as my emotions and energy began to level out, and I stopped having so many emotional breakdowns.

Connie: In contrast, my grief really broke open and went deep last summer when we discovered some things through Todd's best friend that unnerved me and made me angrier than I knew I could be. I'm still trying to work through that, and am in the midst of the forgiveness process.

A dear friend of mine helped me to see this was obviously the season I would enter the grief room Rex had been in from the beginning. I knew I had to be there someday, and that is when it started for me. I wasn't resisting that

depth of grief, but I was surprised it had taken nine
months to get there. And, of course, by then Rex was so
much better.

**How have you stayed close as a couple when you've
grieved so differently and with such different timing?**

Connie: We've learned to honor one another's grieving.
We've learned how to be alone together. Sometimes I
would cry with him and he would thank me. There were
other times when he was crying and I had to leave the
room—times when I felt I could handle a spoonful of pain,
but not the Mack truck of pain Rex was experiencing.

Rex: We did determine to honor each other's personal
process of grieving. But there were times I felt I'd embarrassed her and she was waiting for me to get over it. It did
wear on her, but those things haven't been all that impact-
ing on our relationship in the long run.

Connie: I suppose what has helped me through this is
my stubbornness. I didn't want the enemy to have even a
hint of victory in this. We both determined we wouldn't
allow the enemy to take something as heinous as the loss
of our child and use it to drive us apart.

**As you have talked with other couples who have lost a
child to mental illness and suicide, have you discovered
common thoughts, feelings, fears, and regrets?**

Connie: They say things like, "I didn't do enough . . . I
should have been able to stop this . . . I should have listened more." Guilt is huge. It is like a recording that won't
quit playing, "It's your fault . . . it's your fault."

Rex: Even if you don't assume that full responsibility,
you still have regret. My regret centers on Todd's teen years

and feeling that I wasn't healthy enough emotionally myself to be there for him. Looking back at that tends to haunt me. It is the past, but I think about what could have perhaps been different if I had taken my own emotional well-being seriously.

Connie: But Rex, I thought I was healthy. And as I look back, I think I should have given up my busyness in ministry and attended to Todd more. I think about how I was writing a book, leading worship, and I look back at those things and feel I blew it.

How do you deal with regrets and with other thoughts and emotions that tyrannize you?

Rex: I look to God for the truth of what is and what will be. Recently Connie reminded me of what we are learning about strongholds: They are lies we believe. Sometimes they are half-truths that just leave us short of God's comforting mercy. For example, I journaled last year, "On October 18, I kissed my son goodbye. He was gone a month later."

While there is nothing untrue about this, it leaves me in deep pain over things that I cannot change. Acting on Connie's advice and her prayers for me, I have added to this a layer of truth that is redemptive: "I kissed Todd goodbye for the last time in this world. I will kiss him again in the next."

Connie: I recognize that the enemy is the father of lies and will use any lie, use any stronghold of shame or fear or regret. He'll use anything against me.

The truth is, I did the best I could with what I knew. I have asked Todd's forgiveness even since he's been dead. And I've asked the Lord to forgive me where my priorities

were marked by selfish ambition. That's all I can do. Then
I have to believe what I know about God. That is big:
Reestablishing what I know about God and recognizing
the lies.

**How are you seeing God redeem this loss in your life
and in the lives of others?**

Connie: What we did last week—the Todd-a-thon
[a concert and mental health forum that raised money
to help youth and young adults who battle depression,
bipolar disease, and schizophrenia] was healing for our
souls.

Rex: I've been volunteering at a continuation high
school, spending a few hours a week on campus. It is
partly for them—and, in a big way, for me. One of the
things I believe we'll get to do is raise awareness of screen-
ing tools to identify potential mental health problems earlier. I feel like that would be a tangible contribution
coming out of Todd's death.

Connie: Before Todd died, I knew who I was. With his
death, I lost myself. *Who am I now?*

As we've gotten involved in the lives of so many other
broken people, I discovered that I'm a neighbor—a neighbor in a new community, a neighborhood I wouldn't have
chosen but one chosen for me. So my role is to be a good
neighbor. I just want to be the kind of neighbor that leaves
muffins on your porch when you move in. That is what
God is calling me to now.

We go to a suicide loss support group, and Rex and I
are the only married couple that comes together. We hear
over and over again, "My husband doesn't want to talk
about this." This shows me how important it is to take
time to be alone in your grief, but to come back together.

Rex: Most of the people in the group are divorced. Some are in a new marriage but feel their partner doesn't get it. We hear, "Nobody at home understands me." Most of these people live with a lot of isolation in their grief, which breaks our hearts. Many of the people we're with don't embrace Christianity but they are very attracted to our brokenness and authenticity.

Connie: We're starting to see the fruit and redemption on the other side of the loss. It doesn't bring Todd back, but it enlarges our souls to realize that someone else's life could be spared, enriched, or changed, and that is fuel for us.

But I also have to add that I have wonderful friends who have said, "We just know that you and Rex are going to have spiritual children—an amazing heritage of young people you will mentor."

And I think, *I don't want them. I want Todd.*

There is a hurt part of me that doesn't ever want to replace Todd. Yet there are young people God is putting into our lives—young people who seem to want to be around us and do things with us. That is a stretch for me because it is risk. I've lost once and I can't afford to lose again. But I have to break loose from that safe place where I don't want to hurt anymore. I want to be able to embrace other Todds.

You mentioned people who have tried to comfort you with the promise of spiritual children. Have people said hurtful things to you or have they just avoided you out of awkwardness?

Connie: Some did at first because they didn't know what to say and so they just didn't say anything. Even people we love, some of Todd's friends we're close to, have gone silent at times. I've e-mailed them and said, "Don't let us forget Todd. If you don't help us remember him and all of the funny, unique, wonderful, horrible things he did, how will we remember him?"

That is where we have to remember that other people are still processing the loss of our son. We have to honor their grieving, too. My perfect day would be to gather everybody in a room and let them talk about Todd—but that isn't going to happen.

I'm hurt most often by people who talk about their kids but don't talk about Todd, almost as if they have forgotten that I had a son, too. It breaks my heart.

Rex: Jesus said to rejoice with those who rejoice—and that sounds like the easy part compared to His instruction to weep with those who weep. But on this side of grief, it is harder to rejoice with friends who are rejoicing over children who are doing well and having grandchildren. We have to stretch to celebrate other people's children and to forgive those who've seemingly forgotten Todd.

What would you say to a couple that has just lost a child or another close relative to suicide?

Connie: Come over. Let us sit with you and hug you. We promise not to talk.

Rex: But that might be a vain promise. We just want to be careful with advice we give, remembering how numb we were at the beginning. But once you experience a measure of healing, you tend to just go for it with giving advice.

There are so few things that need to be said. I would pray that we wouldn't say much, but would be present in the room and wait with them.

We would be alone together. That is the best gift you can give to any grieving person.

Chapter Nine

Helping Kids Cope

David and Nancy

We should tell you upfront: We're no parenting experts.

I suppose we're like most parents—doing the best we can at a job that's always changing, a job for which there is mostly on-the-job training.

We've parented one child through grief—one unique child in a unique situation. So this chapter doesn't contain all the answers. What we do have to offer is the most significant lesson we learned about parenting a child through grief. And we've included interviews with several people who know a lot about the subject.

We can remember the point at which we figured out that our son, Matt, was far more likely to follow our example than to follow our instructions. That was a bad day—or should I say a challenging one—because we'd often prefer that he'd do what we say, not what we do.

This reality of parenting is supremely true when it comes to parenting children through grief. Kids follow their parents' lead. What you say matters, but what you live speaks most loudly into your child's life.

When it comes to helping your child recover from the loss of a loved one, the most important influence you have is the example you set in your words, actions, and attitudes.

What Kids Need to Hear and Overhear

Parenting a child through grief began for us that early morning when we told eight-year-old Matt that his sister was going to die. Nancy recorded the conversation in her journal:

December 10, 1998

I've felt so unsure of how to "properly" tell Matt about the diagnosis. This morning, God set up the perfect opportunity and I saw it clearly. I was up doing Hope's 6 A.M. feeding and Matt came down the stairs saying he was cold and couldn't sleep. I asked if he wanted to help me feed Hope so he came to our room and got under the covers between David and me. I knew it was the right time as we were lying there together in the dark.

"Matt, would you like to know what the doctors have told us about Hope?"

"Yes."

"They've explained to us that her cells don't work right. They don't have a way to fix them. And because they don't work right, she probably won't be with us very long."

He started to weep which hurt me deep inside.

"How long?"

"She will probably be gone before you are out of school for the summer."

"Will we have a funeral?"

"Yes, we probably will."

"Can we have another baby?"

"Probably not, because there is such a good chance we would have another baby with this same sickness."

He was so disappointed. I don't think I realized until now how much he really wanted a sibling, and how much I would like for him to have one.

That was a hard conversation. And there were plenty more to come.

Maybe you've had your share, too.

We tend to want to shield our children from hard things, assuming that's best for them. Certainly we don't always have to give our child every detail about suffering or death.

But being straightforward with our children builds trust and shows them respect. Your willingness to face the realities of death and talk about them openly actually gives your child courage and a sense of security. Your child will follow your lead in accepting difficult realities and confronting them with courage and hope.

Facing the hard truths about the death of a family member will cause your child to grow up a little faster than his or her peers. But this maturity is a gift of grief. It is a blessing to learn early that you can face hard things and not be crushed by them.

We soon realized that more important than what we said directly to Matt was what he overheard us say in conversation with other adults, or from a platform. Kids are good at acting like they're not listening when they're really soaking up everything we say. Ever notice how your child hovers nearby when you're whispering on the phone? Kids know that's where they get the straight stuff. What they overhear can feed their confidence that a brighter day is coming, or their dread that the future is grim.

Kids are also stellar hypocrisy-spotters. They can see us telling people we're fine even though we rarely get out of bed. They can see us telling people God is good while we harbor a lot of anger toward Him. They can see us telling people we're handling things well while we're depending on alcohol or some other unhealthy coping mechanism to get through the day.

When we had Hope, and in the months following her death, we were doing a lot of talking about trusting God, about God using this for good, and about our confidence in heaven. At some point it dawned on us that Matt would be able to see if our public claims matched our private discussions and personal experience. We realized he would be able to tell if our talk was a show or for real.

Few of us experience and process the death of someone we love without spiritual and emotional struggle. God gives us the grace we need to stay faithful to Him as we work through our thoughts and feelings. That usually takes some time.

We don't have to hide this process from our children. But we do have to remember that they're following our lead, and the responsibility that gives us. As we come to peace with God over the loss of someone we love, we have to realize that our children are watching. It's up to us to show them what it means for a person of faith to take questions and heartache to God and to look to Him for help and healing.

THE WAY KIDS THINK AND FEEL

Telling Matt that Hope was going to die was hard enough. Telling him he was going to have a little brother—but that this little brother was going to die, too—was unspeakably difficult.

When we turned off the TV and told Matt we needed to talk to him, he knew something was up.

"Matt, you know that we had an operation so we wouldn't have more children," David carefully explained. "But evidently it didn't work, and Mom is pregnant."

Before David could get the rest out, Matt clenched his fist as if to say, "Alright!"

David added, "But this child also has Zellweger Syndrome like Hope had."

Matt's elation was quickly deflated.

"You remember with Hope that it was very hard, and it will be hard again. But you also remember that Hope brought us a lot of joy, and our time with her was rich. And we expect that again, too."

A few minutes later, as it all began to sink in, Matt had a question. It was a question revealing how a child's mind works—or at least how *our* child's mind works.

"Mom, do you think people will bring us meals again like they did while we had Hope?"

"Yes, they probably will," Nancy responded.

"Do you think there's a chance Mrs. Abraham might bring us those stuffed shells she brought us before?"

Yes, kids are kids.

This was one of numerous times throughout our experience that we saw this reality in Matt. In their natural immaturity, children are most concerned with themselves.

While we get worked up about how loss is going to shape them—and we certainly should stay tuned in to their needs—kids can grasp only so much. It all gets filtered through their grid of "How is this going to affect me?"

Perhaps God puts a shield over children's minds and emotions to protect them from sorrow they don't have the maturity to cope with. Maybe He allows them the sorrow that's the right size and shape for a child. They don't have to feel what we as adults feel, and that is a gift.

Children tend to move from one thing to another; in a matter of minutes they can go from deeply missing their sibling or parent to being lost in a video game or wanting to go shopping. They tend not to stay sad for long periods as adults do. They can appear indifferent—ready to go out and play immediately after the funeral.

Play and entertainment give kids a break from their grief. They have the gift of not feeling guilty about continuing to enjoy life in the midst of loss—whereas we adults often struggle with that.

WHAT KIDS WANT MOST

What kids want most is for things to be normal—to not be the center of attention.

Children, and adults who lost a family member as a child, have told us over and over that they hated being pitied by friends and teachers. For Matt, perhaps the worst part of our whole experience was being the center of attention. He didn't like adults asking him what he thought of his sister when she was alive or asking him how he was doing after she died.

Matt didn't know what to say, and it put him on the spot. While children may have the same feelings of grief that adults have, they are usually without the vocabulary to express those feelings. That's awkward for a child.

When we speak publicly about our experience and then invite questions, we can always count on one of the first: "How has all of this affected your son, Matt?" And we find it a bit difficult to answer.

The truth is, we saw little evidence of grief in Matt after Hope died. That concerned us; we wondered if he was holding something in that would affect him negatively later on, or if we were doing something wrong.

We went to see a counselor who specialized in children and grief. She gave us a number of insights and tools that proved very helpful.

One day when the three of us went into the counselor's office, she spread out a large mat that looked like a checkerboard. In each square there was an illustration of an emotion—happy, sad, frustrated, angry, jealous, etc. Then she gave each of us checkers and asked us to place one color in boxes that reflected our own emotions and the other colors in boxes that represented what we thought other people in our family were feeling.

We remember that the game allowed him to reveal that he felt relief. We admitted feeling some, too, which was awkward but true. Having been through intense trauma, we were relieved that the days of anticipating Hope's death were over—even though we missed her.

Making it safe for a child to express conflicting and unwelcome emotions helps him or her move forward. Here, as in every other area, most children follow their parents' lead.

We make it safe for our grieving kids when we openly express thoughts and emotions that may seem unacceptable on the surface. When we're able to question out loud some of the unhealthy or untrue ideas that run through our heads, we free children to admit they've had those thoughts, too.

When we laugh about the foibles of the one who died, or cry about hurts he or she left behind, we help our children deal with reality rather than idealizing the lost loved one. If they sense that the one who died can be spoken of only in the most positive—even superlative—terms, they'll know that any negative remembrance is unwelcome even though it might be healthy to discuss.

KIDS NEED HOPE FOR HEALING

As your children listen to or overhear what you're saying in your grief, what they long most to hear are signs of hope—hope for returned normalcy, for future security. They need reasons to hope that while you may be very sad now, you're on a path toward healing—and that they, too, will not always hurt as much as they hurt right now.

We can't hide all our grief from our children, and we shouldn't try. If you never cry in front of your kids, they might think that if they died you wouldn't miss them or cry for them, either. Your tears are evidence of your love for the person you lost—and for your child.

But neither should we abandon our children by giving ourselves completely over to our grief. In the midst of your sorrow, having one or more children means you still have someone to love and enjoy in your home.

Having children in the house forces us back into normalcy— sometimes before we want to go there. They provide a reason to keep getting up in the morning whether or not we feel like it, a reason to cook a meal and wash the clothes, play a game, and maybe even to laugh now and then.

The tricky balance is to find space to grieve without neglecting the children who depend on you—who probably are grieving in their own way. While we process our loss, we need to stay as fully present for our kids as we can. We need to find ways to show that the loss we feel doesn't erase our joy over having those children here.

We have often wondered how Matt's loss of two siblings will affect him long-term. Time will tell. We've prayed that it will make him compassionate toward those with disabilities and those who experience loss. We see signs of that in his life even now.

We pray that some of the truths we've talked with him about— God's sovereignty in suffering, the value of a less-than-perfect life, our confidence in heaven—have sunk in. More importantly, we hope he's seen us live out what we've talked about. We trust he's noticed that what we believe has made a difference in how we've grieved—that we haven't done it as those who have no hope.

He's following our lead. He's seen us up close in the hardest places of life and the dark days of death. May what he's seen—and what your children see in you—show us all following our Master, walking with Him and toward Him on this difficult pathway called grief.

Helping Kids Get Through Grief

Q&A with Anne Purdy

Anne Purdy has spent 38 years in education, with 20 of those as an elementary school principal. Her childhood experience of loss equips her with unique insight into the struggles kids face in grief.

You have a special compassion for children who are grieving because of your own experience of the loss of your father to leukemia when you were only three years old. What do you remember about that loss that helps you understand what grieving kids are going through?

At first my parents thought my father had the flu, but he was diagnosed with leukemia and was dead six weeks later. But no one told me he died, and I wasn't a part of the funeral process. I was told he was on a long trip.

Months later, I was finally told that my father was dead. I remember going out into the backyard by myself, and telling some other children that my dad was dead. They didn't believe me. "Daddies don't die," they said as they ran away.

I took on the role of feeling responsible for my mom, and for her happiness. I tried not to need mothering and became as self-sufficient as possible. I began having intense fears of losing my mother and recurring nightmares of my mother dying in horrible ways.

One of my survival strategies was to learn to not feel too much. I grew into being strong, tough, resilient, and able to persevere—qualities that are good, but if your heart is not tender you don't love well. One of the things I asked

God for early on was to soften my heart and help me not be afraid to hurt.

When I look back at my first-grade teacher's notes about me, she wrote that I daydreamed and looked out the window all the time. Part of that was my personality, but a lot of it was the grieving process that makes it hard to focus and concentrate. A grieving child has a lot of things on his or her mind.

What are some of the typical effects of grief you see in children?

Children manifest grief so differently than adults do. What looks like anger or sullenness, withdrawal, or melancholy, emotional outbursts, getting into trouble—can actually be manifestations of grief.

And children need to go through the grieving process rather than avoid it. That is the most important work they have to do after a significant loss. Schoolwork is secondary to grief work. They will have to get back to focusing on schoolwork at some point, but first they need the time and space to grieve without the pressure of keeping up and making the grades they used to make in school.

The least amount of time a child needs for grieving a significant loss is about two years. It takes at least that much time for them to begin to function with a back-in-control predictability. They're numb at first and get through on autopilot. The numbness in some ways is God's gift, giving time for the pain to dull before it can be dealt with.

Sometimes children feel a sense of relief that all of the activity and intensity of an illness and funeral is over. They often feel angry and frustrated that they are no longer like everybody else. I often hear them say things like, "I don't like being the kid without the dad" or "the kid without the mom." But I also hear, "I don't like being the adopted kid," or the "smart kid," or the "fat kid." Most children have a strong desire to fit in by being like everyone else, and having a family that is different from most other families can be painful.

What are ways that parents and teachers can help children as they work through their grief?

To sit down with a child and say, "Tell me how you're feeling," will rarely draw out a child. Most likely their answer will be, "I'm fine."

For younger children, I recommend a lot of play together, a lot of side-by-side doing things together, drawing pictures together, reading open-ended books that take you to discussion places—not necessarily books about death, but books that take you deep. You can't always force or coax the needed conversations with children, so it often requires lots of walking and talking, creating opportunities for your child to open up.

It is good for children to see our own grief, which gives them permission to feel sad themselves. As a child who was grieving, I would have loved to have heard my mother say, "I'm really missing Dad today."

I've been awed to see parents who've lost their spouse be honest with their children about how deeply they loved and how much they miss the other parent. I've observed numerous families who have found sweet and special ways to continue to acknowledge that the person who has died is still a valued member of the family. But to get to this healthy place, you have to go through learning how to talk about it in the hard places.

You also have to be careful about talking too much about the person who has died, as hyper-focus causes kids to shut down. It is self-protection. To talk about it all the time hurts too much, and can add to a child's guilt when he is unable to always think or talk about the loss. It is a healthy thing when a child comes to the place he can say, "I was happy today," and not feel bad about it.

My mother worked hard to keep me connected to my father's family who lived on the other side of the country, which helped me feel connected to him. But it was only recently that my mother finally told me things my dad would say about me as a child. I also spent time recently with some men who served with my father in Africa in World War II, and it was comforting to hear stories about him and what he was like.

I wish I had been able to hear these things as a child. To reminisce and rehearse the love the person who died had for the child is helpful, as is reminiscing with other family and friends who knew and loved that person.

Counseling is such a good thing for both children and entire families. Rarely have I seen a carefully selected counselor choice be a negative. Someone who is not so emotionally invested in their own grief can bring perspective and freedom of expression to a child.

Sometimes we as believers are slow to seek out professional counseling because we think that "God and I can do this." But to have a believing counselor help us to work through our thoughts and feelings in the face of loss can be a real blessing.

Helping Kids with Complicated Grief
Q&A with Katherine Koonce

Katherine Koonce, author of Parenting the Way God Parents: Refusing to Recycle Your Parents' Mistakes *(Multnomah, 2006), shares her expertise as a learning specialist and parenting consultant—and her experience of losing her dad to suicide.*

What brought about your own experience of complicated grief?

I grew up with a father who was a very successful businessman, but also an alcoholic and abuser. When I was 17 and had just started college, my father committed suicide. A family friend came to my room and told me they found him and that he was dead, and I started to cry.

And she said immediately, "No, no, no. You cannot cry! You have to be strong for your mother. So get yourself together before you go back in there." So I did.

Busyness was my way of coping. It was ingrained in me early as a way to deal with grief—to keep moving so it doesn't settle on you.

The truth was that I felt a sense of relief that he was gone. But of course I couldn't talk about that.

How do you help children deal with the conflicting feelings they have in a situation of complicated grief?

Mainly by helping them to verbalize what they don't have a vocabulary for on their own, and by being at ease expressing your own conflicting feelings. Don't tell them how to feel. If they don't feel anything, then they don't feel anything. It will happen when it happens.

But speaking and modeling for a child sane and reasonable ways of dealing with feelings is enormously helpful. It helps a child to know he can say things like, "I'm angry that he did that," "I'm sad that I don't have a father," "I'm hurt that he abandoned us."

It is helpful for a child to recognize that you can be sad and also a little happy about the same thing, and that's okay. Differing feelings can coexist. It can really help kids to know that the question, "How do you feel?" doesn't have to have just one answer.

It also helps a child for his or her parent to say, "I might be feeling things you're not feeling, and you might be feeling things I'm not feeling, and that's okay." Children need the permission and the skills to express their conflicting feelings.

What are some of the ways you came to terms with the conflicting emotions and issues in your grief?

Speaking the truth to myself. For example, for a long time I thought mental illness was inevitable for me. I had to speak the truth to myself that mental illness is not inevitable for me or my children—that my identity in Christ is far more powerful than my identity as a member of my family of origin.

Another truth I had to tell myself was, "You could not have done anything to keep him from committing suicide. It was his choice. It wasn't because you let him down or because you were not well-behaved enough or because you didn't say the right things or see the right signals." It is ridiculous to think a child could have prevented the suicide of a parent, but children naturally feel responsible and have to be continually reminded of the truth until it sinks in.

And probably the most important and healing truth I

told myself was the truth of Scripture. I was like a sponge, and memorizing Scripture made a huge difference in my life.

Are there other tools you used to cope with your loss?

One of the most healing things in my experience has been therapy that has taken me back to those painful places in my childhood to visualize Jesus there with me. It helped me to embrace the truth that God had not abandoned me in that place. That imagery—which is really choosing to see reality—helped me recognize that I was never without God. He was always there, and He knows what happened. It helped me to realize that He protected me in a lot of ways.

I also learned to work through my thoughts and feelings with what is called the "sane and reasonable test"—to examine my thoughts and feelings with the question, "Is this sane and reasonable?" If you determine what you're thinking isn't sane or reasonable, you just reject it, and continue to reject it. But if it seems sane and reasonable, you look at it in light of Scripture and ask, "What does God say to me about this?"

What role did other people play in adding to your pain or helping to relieve it?

Learning how to filter out well-meaning things people said that weren't true, sane, or reasonable—especially what older, more established Christians were saying to me—was a huge step for me. One person told me two weeks after my dad's death that my problems were not any worse than anyone else's, and that I just needed to get over myself. Some said I needed to pray more.

But God used the misguided comments of well-meaning

Christians in my life for good. It helped me to think
through carefully what is true in light of Scripture and
what is false religiosity. I came to the place where I could
say, "I do believe the gospel is true and that God has my
heart, but I don't believe what he said and what she
said."

One of the biggest learning experiences has been figuring out who is safe and who is unsafe to talk to. Some people are not safe because they simply haven't had the life
experience to equip them to be a good sounding board. I
also found that when you have suicide or abuse in your
family, some people have a voyeuristic desire to know
more about you because it is so fascinating—not necessarily because they want to be a real friend to you. And to
pour out your story to such a voyeur ends up making you
feel used all over again, and like your life is a freak show.

But I would also have to say that for a while there was
a part of me that wanted to share the dirty details of what
happened in my family because it got people's attention,
and I was desperate for attention. We had been told for so
long we couldn't talk about it, and it felt good to finally
talk about it. When a suicide death occurs, there is no
more pretending, and while that may be awkward and
painful, it can also be freeing.

How has God redeemed the pain and loss in your life?

Well, in every way, really. I feel like whatever has happened to my family and me has made me who I am. I
wouldn't have the capacity to deal with some of the things
I deal with today in other people if I hadn't dealt with that
in childhood.

When you have walked through a period of honest
grief, you experience God in a way you wouldn't wish on

anyone else—but in a way you never could have without the loss. You don't know that when you're going through it. God doesn't immediately say, "This is going to be good," like people often do. He just sits there with you in it and the ministry of His presence is healing. He's not necessarily giving you great pearls of wisdom, but the ministry of His long-term presence is healing.

Helping Boys Through Grief
Q&A with David Thomas, M.S.S.W.

As Director of Counseling for Men and Boys at Daystar Counseling Ministries in Nashville, Tennessee, David does individual, group, and family therapy—specializing in the needs of boys and adolescent males and their families.

In what unique ways does grief manifest itself in boys?

Boys tend to act out their grief, and it tends to come out "sideways." They can't articulate the pain they feel, so it starts coming out in all different directions.

With younger boys it can come out in aggressive ways, like becoming punishing toward a younger sibling or a pet. They have a desire to gain control, and so they take it out on someone or something smaller.

Grieving boys are highly emotional, and have an exaggerated response to minimal things. They can overreact to breaking a toy or losing something of importance to them. Thirdly, they can develop anxiety, phobias, and obsessive-compulsive behaviors.

Adolescents tend to gravitate toward risky behaviors: abusing substances, speeding, or experimenting sexually with girls. Most boys move in and out of grief, not wanting to talk about it for some period of time, perhaps showing no signs of grief at all. And then at some point they fall apart.

So would you say that any boy who has experienced a significant loss needs to see a counselor?

Not necessarily. Oftentimes parents are the ideal voices in the situation, and a professional counselor can coach the parent(s) on what grief looks like, what questions to ask, when to best engage kids, and help them understand what is normal.

It is very natural and common for kids to regress in their grief and to want to sleep in the bed with parents, talk babyish, regress in their behavior as a way of seeking safety, comfort, and attention. That is not anything to have great concern about initially. It really is normal.

Get concerned when they don't come out of those behaviors at some point, or they become more exaggerated. Loss can halt a child's emotional development. If it doesn't jump-start itself naturally, which it does the majority of the time, we want to intervene to help that process get going, and counseling is a primary tool for that.

How can parents get boys and young men to start talking, since they tend to keep their thoughts and feelings to themselves?

The best tool a parent can use to draw boys out is to talk out of their own experience and openly share their own thoughts and questions. This shows kids it is safe and good to talk about grief. But sitting down eye-to-eye for a big conversation can be threatening to most boys.

I recommend that parents maximize bedtime. The barriers are down as they lay in bed in the dark, and kids become more thoughtful and responsive. Kids are more vulnerable emotionally late at night. Parents can also go on a drive together or hike together. Talking about these important issues and feelings around a task or activity is likely to bring boys out.

Parents need to continue to give them opportunities to ask questions, although 8 out of 10 times boys won't open up. This is when a parent might say, "I know you didn't have any questions last time we talked, but maybe you do now."

What do boys especially need while they are going through grief?

Kids need a lot of reassurance when their parents are grieving. I met recently with a young man whose mom is very emotional because of grief. He told his mom, "I hate it when you cry all the time. I never come in the house that you haven't been crying."

And in that statement to his mom he is saying that because his mother has always been the most stable presence in his home, he doesn't know what to do when she isn't emotionally stable. His fear is that he needs to be taking care of her and he has no idea how to do it.

In this case, it is appropriate for her to say something like, "I know this must be hard for you, but I am going to be sad because what happened is so sad and so scary, so it is right that I'm sad. But you don't have to figure out how to make me feel better or how to make me stop crying. That is just what I'm going to do at this point. And even though I'm really sad, I'm still fully capable of being your mom."

Kids experience reassurance through words and also

through ritual, and a return to normalcy. Parents are often surprised when their kids want to go back to school the next day after someone dies. And I say, "Actually that's great! Loss is chaotic, and he wants something normal."

Oftentimes kids ask parents to call the school and instruct the adults and other kids not to ask about what has happened. They say, "I don't want one more person to say, 'I'm so sorry,' or ask, 'How are you?'" They want the relief of not having every moment and their whole identity defined by their loss.

What are some traps parents fall into as they try to parent their sons through grief?

First and foremost, parents should not demand that a boy show grief or be willing to talk about it at length and often. Parents often think their son never cries when the reality may be that he does cry when he's alone. Grief looks different for kids than for adults. The opposite mistake is never giving the child an opportunity to talk about his grief at all.

Secondly, some families force the idea of heaven on a grieving child as if that should instantly take away their sadness and their questions. If you think about how hard it is as adults to get our hearts and minds around our questions about why God allowed the person we love to die, how much more must kids wrestle to make sense of things? Families of faith can sometimes force the concept of heaven, rather than allowing kids to get to that place of acceptance on their own.

One young man I counseled told me that his grandparents continually said about his brother who had died, "He's in a better place."

And the boy wanted to scream in response, "I know that is true, but I'm sick of hearing it and I'm furious and sad that I don't have my brother!"

It is very healthy for parents to show their grief, which is modeling something useful. But they have to be careful they don't shift their child into a role of caretaking. Parents make a huge mistake when they allow their kids to assume responsibility for the parents' happiness.

It can also be damaging to kids to idealize the person who died, forgetting or ignoring that person's character flaws. We want to help create a realistic memory that includes both strengths and weaknesses.

Humor is key. Boys especially respond well to humor. Something like, "Remember how your brother used to make you so mad when he would come into your room and take your stuff?"

Children who have lost a sibling especially need to know that their parents remember the child who has died in reality—so that they don't feel like they have to compete with the memory of a perfect person.

A lot of your patients are in group therapy. What is that like, and what are the benefits of group therapy for a child or adolescent who is grieving?

First, it is so normal that a child wouldn't want to go. I usually say to kids when they come in, "I don't blame you at all for not wanting to be here, because you're not sure what you're getting into. Ask me questions you want to know."

Boys often ask if everybody is going to sit around and talk about their feelings and cry. I say, "Come try it out a couple of times and see what it is like."

Many times a boy's resistance is really a fear they are going to blubber and lose control of themselves. So we talk about it. I tell kids they don't have to say a word. But then they naturally open up as they hear other guys tell their stories.

At the agency where I work, we have a very back-door approach. I have toys and gadgets in my office and get the kids just talking about their day, which graduates into a deeper conversation.

There was one girl who was approached by someone who said, "I heard you went to counseling."

And she said, "No, I don't. I go to Daystar to talk, but I don't go for counseling."

I really like that. That is our goal.

Group therapy is a powerful tool for adolescents during the period of their development when the voice of their peers is so strong. They benefit from hearing somebody else put words to what loss feels like in ways they can't, and in ways adults can't. To hear about loss from the voice of another peer is so very powerful.

You Don't Have to Be Strong

Q&A with Rachel Robbins

At this writing, Rachel Robbins is a college freshman who lost her dad eight years ago. He died suddenly on Father's Day as they were playing softball in the front yard.

What stands out to you as you think back to what it was like to lose your dad as an elementary-aged girl?

It happened so fast. He fell, and all of a sudden he was in the hospital, and then he was gone. Sometimes I wish I could go back and see it all slower.

My mom didn't want me to see his body in the casket, but I really wanted to because I didn't get to say good-bye—and so she agreed.

I went out and bought a two-part pendant and put one part in his hand in the casket with him, and I have the other half. It was weird that his hand was so cold and stiff—that part was scary and I didn't like it.

But it means a lot to me that we share that special thing between us that no one else shares, and that I got to say goodbye to him and tell him that I love him. It also really helped me to look at his face and see for myself that he was not in pain and that there wasn't blood anywhere, because as a child I just didn't know.

What I remember most about the funeral process was all these old people crowding around me who would see me and start crying. They would ask me questions and I didn't know what to say. It was all very awkward. I just wanted to be alone with my family and my mom.

It took me a long time to realize that he was never coming back. It just didn't sink in for a few weeks. There were so many people at our house all the time, and a part of me thought that maybe if they left we'd start to get back to normal and then he'd come back. What I wanted most was for things to go back to being normal again.

What was the grief experience like for you?

I felt very protective of my mom, and I decided early on I didn't want her to see me cry—ever. I knew it was so hard for her and that she had cried so much.

And I knew that if she saw me cry, it would make her cry more, and I didn't want that. One time I went up to my bed and was crying, and she came in my room and started crying with me. I decided I could never let that happen again.

I wanted things to be perfect for my mom. I thought if they were perfect for her then she wouldn't be sad, and that was the goal. So I tried to control my brother and sister so they wouldn't cry or fight or add to her sadness. I tried to keep the house cleaned up all the time so it wouldn't add to her stress.

After we started going to church again, I started to get angry. It was hard going to church when people were whispering, "That's the girl who lost her dad." It was hard to see complete families when I felt like we were not a whole family because we were missing somebody. I remember yelling at God and crying on my bed, "Who do You think You are, and why would You do this to me?"

So when did you finally let yourself cry and grieve?

It wasn't until I started counseling maybe seven months after my dad died that I really began to grieve. I didn't like the first counselor. I liked talking to someone about my dad, but I just didn't connect with her. So my mom found another counselor, and there I felt free to talk about it in one-on-one and counseling, and with a group of other kids my age.

Being a part of the group showed me that there are other kids like me going through the same thing I was going through. I wasn't on my own. Seeing that there were other people my age who have similar pain made a huge difference.

In middle school, because I didn't have any male figures in my life, I became completely boy crazy. I would go after whatever boy whose attention I could get. I just wanted to have a boyfriend.

I'm sure that at the time I couldn't say that I was "psychologically deprived of a male figure," but now I can see it clearly. I was hungry for a male influence to tell me, "I like you. You're pretty." I wasn't mature in my walk with God. I hadn't learned yet to depend on Him to meet my needs.

How did you come to that place of learning to depend on God?

In ninth grade things were very hard at home, and I just wanted something stable in my life. I knew the only thing that would make me stable was God. So I worked hard on my relationship with God, and found out who I am in Christ.

So many other kids who haven't gone through something like I have gone through don't really run to God, because they haven't had anything that forced them in that direction.

Are there other ways you can see how God has used this loss for good?

First, my mom is my best friend, and she is good at balancing that with being my mom. That wouldn't have happened if my dad were still here. Our relationship is such a blessing, and I see that so many of my friends don't have that with their moms.

And secondly, I see how God has used this loss to make me into the person I am. I had to grow up fast. I'm a lot more mature than friends my age because they've never experienced a loss.

One of the reasons I'm not a partier—going out drinking and having sex—is that I have a better perspective on life because I grew up and matured quicker. I don't run to those things because I've been through pain and I know those things aren't going to help me. Instead I think, *That is not going to do anything for me; why would I put that in my life?*

I have more perspective on things. For example, if I get a bad grade, I'm not completely lost or frantic.

But all that doesn't mean that I don't really miss my dad and wish he were here. I especially feel it on special occasions, like when the father-daughter dance came around every year, at graduation, and when I moved into college. Christmas is still hard.

It is not an everyday thing, but tonight is a good example. We have a guy coming over to fix our computer, and I wish my dad were here because he could take care of that. There are so many times I feel like life would be easier if my dad were still here.

What advice would you give to someone like yourself who has just lost a parent?

Don't try to be so strong. It's okay to cry and be sad. You've lost someone very important to you and it is right to be sad about that.

But also know that in time you will be okay. After a while it won't hurt so much or so much of the time.

It's also okay to feel scared. As someone who just lost a parent, it's normal to be scared and feel weak and it doesn't mean that you are stupid or abnormal.

Sometimes I would "ask" my dad, in my mind, "Why did you leave me?" It took time to understand that he didn't leave me on purpose. Your parent didn't leave you on purpose. He or she didn't choose to leave you, and there is nothing you could have done to stop or prevent him from passing away.

I remember people always telling me, "You're going to

be fine." And I didn't like that. I wanted to scream. But when people say things like this, you have to remember that they are not trying to hurt you in any way or make you mad. They are trying to tell you they love you and are there for you, just not in the right words. They are also trying to give you hope in what seems to be a hopeless situation.

And instead of dwelling only on the fact that your parent isn't here anymore, remember all the good memories and fun times you had together—and find happiness in them.

And what advice would you give to the parent who has lost his or her spouse?

Don't rush into getting married again anytime soon. Even though I don't want my mom to be alone, I'm so glad she didn't start dating or get married again quickly.

So many of the widows my mom walks with are married again within a year or two, and they don't realize how hard that is for a child to adjust to. As a parent who has lost their partner, they might look at the situation and see their child without a father or mother and think he just needs a dad or mom.

But that is not what the child needs or wants. When a child says, "I miss Dad," that doesn't mean he wants to replace him as soon as possible.

Also, I would say take your child to counseling even if they don't really want to go. I am so glad my mom put up with all my whining and took me to a counselor, and then worked to find another counselor when I couldn't relate to the first one.

I think some people might not take their kids to counseling because they think that means they have failed themselves as a parent. But as a child or teenager, we don't always understand the emotions we're feeling, and we're confused about the whole situation.

We can't always talk to our parents about what we're thinking and feeling, and we can't talk to our friends about it because they don't understand and they usually act awkward when we bring it up. We're afraid that if we talk honestly to other grown-ups that we know, like a pastor, teacher, or relative, they might tell our parent what we've confided in them.

It is much easier to talk to a counselor who can help us understand what we are feeling and why we're feeling that way, and just listen to us talk without a biased opinion.

Something my mom did that was helpful was that she put pictures up around the house that were action shots of my dad and me and my dad and our family doing fun things together, instead of only posed photographs. I think if she had put up only posed photographs of the whole family, it would have made me sad as I would have looked at them and seen only that someone was missing from our family. With the action shots, I was able to focus on the fun times I had with my dad, and it brought a smile to my face.

Chapter Ten

Birthdays, Deathdays, and Holidays

Nancy

Walking with a friend in the park the other morning, I told her that Hope would have been eight years old this week. She asked me what it's like for me on Hope's and Gabe's birthdays. I told her it varies widely.

When those days come around, I usually can find a way—sometimes very small and sometimes more significant—to celebrate their lives. I'm grateful they were here, if for only a short time, so I can find joy in that.

I celebrate the impact they had on other people, even with their limitations and the brevity of their lives. With gratitude I remember the joy and richness they brought, the gifts they gave us in the form of a deeper understanding of God and deeper relationships with people.

But I must quickly add that in the time surrounding their birthdays I'm especially sensitive. Tears come much more easily, as if they were just waiting beneath the surface to be released. There is a deep longing to have Hope and Gabe here, and a deep disappointment that they are not.

Sometimes I'm able to stuff the feelings inside until the date passes and life goes on. And sometimes it sneaks up on me and comes out in sobs.

I also told my friend that as creative as I sometimes am in finding meaningful ways to celebrate those birthdays, it's desperately difficult to come up with a good way to mark the deathdays. I usually find myself wishing I could crawl into a hole until the date passes and it's safe to emerge.

But if I'm honest, I sometimes think the deathdays are hard because on those days I focus on myself and not on Hope and Gabe. I remember what it felt like for me to hold their lifeless bodies, to hand them over, to put their bodies into the ground and go on.

I'm very sad for myself on those days as I remember the trauma and loss. What seems vague to others when I say, "My child died," is not a vague memory to me. As I remember the details, the emptiness comes rushing back with a force that takes my breath away.

But when I say the deathdays are hard, it's more that the *anticipation* of the days is hard. For me, the day itself is often not so bad. It's during the time leading up to it, when it seems death is coming again and I can't stop it, that I'm filled with a sense of dread and helplessness.

FINDING WAYS TO CELEBRATE A LIFE

Birthdays, deathdays. Sometimes I feel they're always coming at me.

It's hard to know what to do with these days, isn't it? Letting them just go by doesn't seem right. Yet it can be so hard to work up the energy to get out of bed, let alone do something constructive or meaningful.

At one time I would have said that the key to getting through these days is to have a plan. But I'm not so sure about that anymore. As these days have come and gone throughout the years, I've realized that I often don't know how I'm going to feel. And I really don't want the pressure of following through on a plan.

So I just look for ways to draw Hope and Gabe close in my memory—and minister to others *in* their memory.

Some years we've pulled out pictures and videos. Some years we've visited the grave. Some years we've simply said something like this during the day: "Hope would be eight years old today." And we smile.

Usually a friend or two will send me an e-mail or flowers, and I'm moved to tears that they haven't forgotten.

On what would have been Gabe's fourth birthday, I made a birthday cake. Having uncovered a numeral-four candle under old napkins and paper plates in the cabinets, I figured it was meant to be.

Some people might think that's a little weird. But finding some small way to mark these days as a family seems to relieve the pressure. Often everyone is thinking about it, but it's hard to know how to bring it up. Something simple—making a cake, lighting a candle, tying a ribbon around a memorial tree, going out to your loved one's favorite restaurant, inviting people over who loved him or her as you did—can help your family mark the day in a meaningful way.

Probably the most meaningful thing I do to observe these birthdays is writing a check to the memorial fund that bears the names of Hope and Gabe. It benefits special-needs students at the school they would have attended with Matt. This birthday gift does something good for somebody else—and extends the legacy of Hope's and Gabe's lives in a fruitful rather than simply sentimental way.

On what would have been Hope's fifth birthday, I had a big party. I put on display some reminders of how God had used her life and Gabe's to help others. It was a celebration of the meaning with which God, in His grace, had infused their lives.

Coming up with a way to celebrate together the impact of a life helps a family live out the "working all things together for good" that Romans 8:28 promises. It creates an appointed time to check in on each other's grief and gain perspective as a family on your loss.

What are birthdays but a celebration of life? When we know

that the life of the one we love goes on in the ultimate celebration in heaven, we can join in the singing, grab hold of the joy.

As for deathdays—they're birthdays, too, in a sense. For those who belong to God's family, these days commemorate being birthed into God's presence—where life as it was meant to be truly begins.

HANDLING THE HOLIDAYS

"Happy Thanksgiving!"

"Merry Christmas!"

"Happy New Year!"

As the end of the year approaches, everywhere we turn someone is telling us we should be happy!

But for families who've recently lost someone they love, the holidays can seem more like something to survive than to enjoy. The traditions and events that can add so much joy and meaning to the season are punctuated with painful, repeated reminders of our loss. Many of us wish we could find a quiet place to hide until January 2.

Since we likely can't hide away, it makes sense to have a strategy as we approach the holiday season. We need a plan that will help us get through what can be a very difficult time of year.

Hope was born on a Monday before Thanksgiving. I thought we'd always be celebrating her birthday around that holiday. In a sense we do—but of course it's not the way I thought it would be.

When that first Thanksgiving rolled around six months after Hope died, I was in the lowest part of my grief. I couldn't bear to do a big family thing, fearing that perhaps no one would say her name or that I wouldn't have space to just be sad. But we didn't want to stay home in our quiet house and feel the gloom closing in, either.

We felt we needed to do something completely different, make a new memory. So we drove to Asheville, North Carolina, stayed in a bed-and-breakfast, visited the Biltmore mansion, and went to the movies.

We did have some fun, though our sadness came along for the ride. Still, we did our best to pursue joy and celebrate life together in new and different ways. The change of scenery lightened our load of sorrow.

Shortly before making the trip, I went by a friend's house. She was one of those people who never seemed to really "get" our loss, and seemed to want me to hurry back to being happy. When I told her about our plans, she said, "That should be fun!" The look she gave me said I was supposed to agree wholeheartedly with her.

"Yes, it should," I said.

I didn't know how to explain that when you've lost a member of your family, even the best of times are painfully incomplete. Someone is missing. Even the best days, the happiest events, are tinged with sadness.

Holidays raise hard questions for grieving families. How do you get a Christmas tree without Dad, when he always picked out the best one? How does a child find a gift for Dad without Mom there to help? How does a wife get through New Year's Eve with no one to kiss at the stroke of midnight?

There are no simple answers, no easy ways to get through these important, memory-laden days. But there are a few things that can help bring back some joy amidst the sadness.

START A NEW TRADITION

My parents love to have all their kids at their house for holidays, but they're supportive and flexible and have never laid a guilt trip on any of us when we've made other plans.

Many of my friends don't have it so good. They would never think of not meeting their family's holiday expectations. They often find themselves building their plans around those expectations rather than around what's best for their own immediate family.

When you're grieving the loss of someone who isn't at the table, it can be especially hard to move through traditional holiday family events. Perhaps this is the year to break with tradition, do something different, make a new memory.

Every family has holiday assumptions; some see them as rigid rules that can't be broken. But part of taking care of your family right now may mean not making the expected trip, not participating in the usual rituals, not showing up at the big dinner. That's okay.

Besides crossing things off your list that you don't want to do this year, perhaps there are some new things you want to try—particularly things that will honor the memory of the one you've lost.

For example, do you want to give a gift to someone who played an important role in your loved one's life? Do you want to buy a tree you can plant in the yard as an ongoing reminder of hope and healing in the years to come? Do you want to make a donation to a charity or ministry in your loved one's honor?

Surround Yourself with Comfort

When we're grieving, we quickly find out who's willing to share our sorrow and give us time to be sad. We also discover who's uncomfortable with our tears, wanting us to "get over it."

Certain relatives or friends you see during the holidays may add to your pain with too many words or by never talking about your family's loss. While you don't want your relationships to be forever ruled by your sensitivity, for a little while you may need to avoid those who add to your hurt.

This may be the holiday season to do what brings you comfort. So if being with your family and continuing tradition brings the soothing you need, do it. But if your extended family is insensitive to your grief, you may choose this year to be around people you can count on to understand your sorrow, people who offer the emotional and spiritual support you need to get through the season.

Invite someone over who helps you remember your loved one. Or slip away occasionally from the family reunion to call someone who supports you.

Maybe you need to communicate clearly to your extended family what will bring you comfort. You can't expect them to know. If you long to hear your loved one's name, explain that you look forward to a time of talking together about him. Or set the tone by bringing up her name yourself. You'll break the ice for everyone else who's thinking of your loved one—but isn't sure whether saying his name will make you feel better or add to your sadness.

Holiday traditions are meant to add joy and meaning. If this year they only seem like another heavy burden, leave the decorations packed up. Don't send out the cards. If the weight of grief makes travel harder this year, perhaps you don't need to make the trip.

On the other hand, adding cheer to your usual surroundings—or getting away from them—might feel really good. There may be some tears as you and your family put the ornaments on the tree, but they may help to release some of your disappointment over the fact that the person you love is not here this year. You may not relish the work of getting out a family Christmas card—especially taking a group photo with someone glaringly missing. But sharing your loss and honoring your loved one through holiday communication might be the perfect way to bring some joy back into the season.

Expect to Feel Sad, but Be Open to Joy

When I remember that first Christmas after Hope died, I picture myself standing at the sink preparing Christmas dinner—with tears running down my face. The void was enormous. Tears were the only way to release the pain I felt.

There's no avoiding sadness when our hearts are broken, but neither is there a complete absence of joy. Sometimes I think we're afraid to feel joy when we're grieving; it can feel like a betrayal to be happy. Or we fear that if we're too happy, those around us will think we're officially "over it" and our sorrow will no longer be tolerated.

Experiencing sorrow doesn't eliminate joy. In fact, I've come to think that sorrow actually increases our capacity for joy. As our lows are lower, our highs are higher. Deep sorrow expands our ability to feel all emotions deeply.

PREPARE YOURSELF FOR HEALING
IN THE COMING YEAR

My worst New Year's Eve was the one when we had Hope.

Our small group was at our house, celebrating the occasion. I found I had to slip away to my bedroom. I pulled the covers over my head, holding Hope in my arms, wanting to wish away the entrance of another year.

Everyone on the other side of the house was wishing each other, "Happy New Year!" I knew the coming year was going to be the saddest of my life—the year I would have to bury my daughter.

When the next New Year's Eve came around, it felt painful once again. I was leaving behind the year in which I had known Hope. The milestone of the new year was a reminder that time was moving on, taking me further away from her.

But a new year is a new beginning. And God is a God of new beginnings. He is at work in us in each new year, healing and renewing and remaking. And He works through His Word.

While your family's holiday seasons likely will be sprinkled with occasional pain, these times can also be an opportunity to discover God in ways that you might not have been hungry for without the hurt of losing someone.

Your family may not have had a habit of reading the Bible together or praying together before your loss. Perhaps the holiday season will give you the opportunity to read God's Word as a family, using an Advent guide or devotional as Christmas approaches.

And you don't have to stop there. Perhaps the new year will prompt a resolution to begin setting aside time to allow God to speak into your lives, into your sorrow and questions. You might consider using a daily devotional such as *The One Year Book of Hope*, which I wrote specifically to help grieving people get into God's Word. I regularly hear from couples who read it together, and even long-distance relatives who read it together each day over the phone.

The practice of reading and talking about God's Word as a family is hard to get going—and even harder to *keep* going. But so much has changed in your household, this season could be the right time to start.

You don't have to hide during this holiday season, waiting for it to pass. You can choose to take care of yourself and prepare yourself for healing in the coming year.

Your family can enter into the Nativity with your sorrow and need and discover in a new way why the angel proclaimed, "Do not be afraid. I bring you good news of great joy that will be for all the people" (Luke 2:10).

Feeling Like a Family Again

Q&A with Bill Lee

When Bill Lee's wife, Carol Ann, died after a horse-riding accident, he and his four children wondered if their family would forever feel incomplete.

What do you remember about your initial thoughts and feelings after Carol Ann died?

I remember mainly the overwhelming sense that I had no idea what I was going to do. I stood at the hospital thinking, *What am I going to do? What will I do with my kids? How will I run my company? Who will fix supper?*

It was completely overwhelming. I remember saying, "God, You are going to have to give me what I need to do this because it is overwhelming to think about what life ahead holds for me."

When I walked in the church for the visitation and saw Carol Ann's casket for the first time and my four kids sitting in front of it on the front row I thought, *God, I can't do this.*

My experience has been that when I have come against the things that I felt I just could not handle, God has met me, and there has been grace for that moment. Over time I began to believe that it would happen every time. Ultimately I have come to the point I'm at today, which is: While I don't want anything bad to happen to me again, if it does, I have no doubt that God will show up for me.

In addition to your own grief over losing Carol Ann, you had four children who were grieving. How did you help them through that?

I went to a pediatric counselor and said, "These are my four children and their ages and how they are processing the loss." She would spend hours talking to me about each one of them. Then I would go back and put her advice into practice.

The counselor said one of the important things about grieving in front of your children is that they can learn to release their grief by watching you do it.

I felt a real responsibility to help them do their grief right, and it was hard because I wanted to do my own grieving. But I think I vicariously grieved through my kids, and we grieved together. We cried together.

We'd eat dinner and there was nobody in her chair, and we'd talk about that. I'm a big believer that if everybody's thinking it, then somebody ought to say it.

I also made sure each child had an adult they could talk to besides me. For example, my oldest daughter was running track and I asked her coach, "Would you be the one? It's not anything formal. She doesn't know I'm asking, but for a few months would you be intentional to spend time with her, and invite her to talk about her mom?"

Carol Ann died during the summer when there was no school, and I was able to take six weeks off from work to just be at home with them. So every day I did something with each kid for an hour individually—four-wheeling with Jacob, horse riding with Sarah. I would tell them how bad it was for me, how hard it was. Some of the most profound times I've had with my children were in those times.

One day I took Caleb to a dock where I had often gone with Carol Ann, and I told him about how she and I would sometimes get a babysitter and drive down the road and come there when the kids thought we were going out

somewhere. We laughed about that, and I said, "But everything is different now."

He said, "You know, Dad, the air feels different to me."

And I said, "It does to me, too. Everything feels
different."

**What are some of the significant ways things were
different?**

In a weird sense we felt like we didn't have a whole
family anymore. I remember getting a card in the mail that
said, "God has a plan for your family," and when I opened
it I looked at it and thought, "We don't have a family anymore!" And my kids felt the same way.

I remember when, early on, one of my sons said,
"We'll probably never go on vacation again."

I told them, "I know that you can't believe that we will
go on vacation again, but I'm telling you right now that
there will come a day when we go on vacation again, and
you will enjoy it. I know you can't believe it right now."

I knew God was going to heal us individually and as a
family. But I don't think I anticipated He would heal us to
the place that we're healed today.

**How did you deal with the very practical aspects of
having four children and no wife and mother at home
anymore?**

I was really fortunate that I have a lot of family close
by. And a benefit of being in the Body of Christ is that you
have that Body around you. For two years there was a
meal waiting for us for supper every night, prepared and
delivered by someone in the Body. My mom came to my
house every morning for five years to get breakfast and get
the kids off to school.

Ultimately my sister became sort of a nanny. She comes every day, is there when my kids come home from school, fixes supper, and leaves right before I get home.

I was fortunate to have several women who wanted to be surrogate moms to my kids. I had to be careful that they were married and that their husbands were my friends. And I figured out quickly that it wasn't a good idea to have young, unmarried women in the house. I didn't need the risk of somebody falling in love.

But while I did get a lot of help, at first I wanted the kids to know that I could take care of them. One of the first things my kids said after Carol Ann died was, "How are we going to eat? Who is going to fix supper?"

So I worked hard to let them know that I could take care of them. I took and picked them up from school for the first year. While there was someone bringing us meals, I cleaned up, I did laundry, I went to their games, and I went to dentist appointments. I played the mom role for a year.

I wanted them to know, "*We* can do this. You will be taken care of. You don't have anything to worry about as far as the logistics of life."

When you talk with men who've recently lost their wives, what do they want to know from you?

Men want to know, "Am I going to feel better? Is this pain going to go away?" You feel so much pain and a sense that life will never be the same. And the truth is, it never is. I lost a part of my life I'm never going to get back.

Early on I remember telling people it felt like I lost a leg. I was going to learn to walk again, but I would never have my leg back. In some ways that is still true, but I don't feel exactly that way anymore. I feel like my leg is

going to grow back. It will be different and I will notice
the difference, but I do not have to spend the rest of my
life with this gaping hole and hurt in my life.

**What is the difference between men you've met with
who never seem to get better and those who still hurt
but also heal?**

Those who heal do so because they choose to believe
God's promises. They believe it when God promises, "I will
never leave you or forsake you," that "all things will work
for good for those who love the Lord and are called," that
"suffering produces perseverance, which produces character, which produces hope and it doesn't disappoint you."

They embrace the transformation process that happens
when we bring our pain to God and say, *I believe You and I
will continue to believe You till the day I die.*

But it's hard to have that kind of belief if you don't
really have a relationship with God to start with. If you
had never made any effort to know Him before you
encountered the grief, you can't just drum that up
instantly.

But He will meet you where you are. If a person
decides to believe God's promises and decides to trust
God's promises no matter what, that is what enables him
to walk through grief and come out on the other side
strong and whole.

It is enticing to think when you begin to really hurt
that the answer to the pain will be to bring another
woman into that empty place as soon as possible. But men
need to give themselves time to really grieve. You can let
the Lord be in your process, but there has to be a process.
You have to be intentional about grief, and accept that it's a
long, painful process.

Moving quickly into another relationship was out of the question for me. I knew it would mess up my kids, who already had so much to deal with. I decided early on I wouldn't rock their boat any more than it had already been rocked.

I date occasionally and they know it and are fine with it, but they still don't want me to get married—at least not right now. "Wait till we go to college," they've said. And I probably will.

What do you see in your kids' lives that shows you God is redeeming this incredible loss?

In my 20-year-old daughter I've seen that it has given her perspective. Little things don't rattle her because she has been through tremendous difficulty and knows the difference. She knows everything is going to be okay and that she's going to be fine.

My children are whole—almost more so than other kids that haven't been through what we've been through.

Our family has pulled together because we've needed each other. We went from being a typical family with the kids fighting about who is going to sit in the front seat—to a family that was focused on taking care of each other. And that is a nice thing for my kids to take into adulthood.

They also have embraced that this loss has been purposeful. My daughter said recently that she feels set apart or chosen for this and by this. I tell my kids, "Most kids will never feel what you're feeling, and really, that is a gift in your life. Right now it is painful, but one day it will be powerful if God can get hold of you in this process. That is what is hopeful. You may curse the process, but it's an opportunity."

How about you? How has this loss changed you?

Early on I knew I wanted to be grateful in the midst of my grief, but I wrestled with it. That first Thanksgiving after Carol Ann died, we were standing around the table at her parents' house and I remember my father-in-law saying, "We have so much to be grateful for."

And I thought, *You have lost your mind!* It was so offensive to me. But on the other hand, I genuinely wanted to feel that. I wanted to be grateful for what I had and I started reminding myself of what I had. It was a struggle. But I discovered that gratitude is what incubates hope.

The experience of losing Carol Ann has also instilled in me a determination to persevere. Now I think about heaven, eternity, and the brevity of life. I think about how soon I'll be there, how awesome it will be, how worthwhile the wait is. And I figure I can do anything till then. I have a real sense that my life is not that long, that these are light and momentary afflictions, and it makes them more bearable.

I had a lot of fear early on, but a mind-set that life is short gives you courage. You think, *Surely this is for something significant. I might as well go for it. So, God, use this to change me. Let it propel me to invest my life in something important.*

Do you still feel like you are no longer a complete family?

Christmas has always been bittersweet. Early on they were mostly bitter with a thread of sweetness. But over the years, the sweetness begins to be stronger until it becomes more sweet than bitter. Christmas this year was still bittersweet—still wishing that Carol Ann were here, but so sweet.

This past Christmas Eve morning my oldest daughter came down, and we had coffee together and talked about how hard it is to believe that we can feel so good—so hopeful, so healed, so whole. And that we can have so much fun, so much laughter, so much to look forward to— that the Christmas holidays can be so special and seem so complete.

It feels complete. We feel like a complete family, like everything is in place. Nothing is missing.

Chapter Eleven

Remembering

Nancy

For years I'd felt like it was time. Last week we finally did it.

We had the room painted—the one we've always called "Hope's room," even though she never spent a night in it.

It had been beautifully and lovingly painted eight years ago by my friend Evie, before Hope was born. There were verses from the Psalms written on the walls amidst a smiling sun, under a ceiling of clouds. I called it my Psalm 8 nursery; to me it was the most beautiful nursery that never served that purpose.

Even though Evie's design had stayed on the walls all these years, the space was turned back into a guest room long ago. I wrote about it in my journal that difficult day—October 15, 1999.

I feel so torn today. A couple of weeks ago, I went through Hope's things and sent a package to Judy who wants to put together a scrapbook of her life. I had a great time doing it really. I think the scrapbook is going to be such a joy to look through.

It was the first step in getting ready to get her room more in order, and I've been thinking toward doing that today, partly because I've been expecting my parents might come this weekend. They called last night, and they will be here tonight.

Somehow the idea of her room becoming our guest room again tonight is a sense of coming full circle. I don't really have the words to put to it, but it just hurts.

I don't want to be one of those moms who leaves a child's room as he or she left it to become a shrine. Besides, Hope never really used that room since she slept in our room her entire short life. But it is HER room. And allowing anybody to take it over—even if it is my parents, and even if it is only for a couple of nights—just feels like a sacrifice. It wasn't supposed to be a guest room anymore.

That night all I could think about was how hard it was for me. But as I write, I realize for the first time how hard it must have been for my parents. They were still letting go of the dream of having a beautiful granddaughter; sleeping in what was supposed to be her room must have rubbed in the loss in a painful way.

What to Do with the Stuff?

When I was pregnant with Gabe, my friends wanted to have a baby shower for me. I begged them not to.

One of the hardest things in the months after Hope died was figuring out what to do with all the stuff—clothes, gifts, equipment, notes, and cards—so much everywhere I turned that I didn't want to discard but didn't know what to do with.

I just didn't want to face that again after Gabe died. So the gift they gave me was an open house for people to meet Gabe and give to a portrait fund.

It's hard to know what to do with the stuff, isn't it? Especially the very personal things—your wife's jewelry, your husband's razor, your child's favorite toy.

I remember being at the home of friends after they came home from the hospital, where their daughter had died suddenly and unexpectedly. The girl's fingerprints were still on the window; they struggled with whether or not they should wipe them away. How we want to hold on to the precious reminders of the ones we love!

It's hard to find the right balance when it comes to items that help us remember those we miss so much. How do we memorialize someone we love without slipping over the edge into shrine-building?

Some homes can seem like shrines dedicated to someone who has died. There is a sense in the house that time stopped when the person died, and that changing anything would be desecrating the sacred.

A week or so after the funeral for her son, Hunter, my friend Jill Kelly and I talked about shrines. Jill was feeling an extreme need to have pictures of Hunter all around the house, in every room. Because he was no longer there, and the void was so stinging, to see pictures of him was a tremendous comfort. But we also discussed the "weirdness" of allowing a house to become a shrine to someone who has died.

I think the temptation to create a shrine is greatest when the loss is fresh. The photos and remembrances are such a comfort, helping us to transition into life without the real and living person. We want to honor our loved one, and remind the world that's going on around us that someone significant is missing.

So we have huge portraits framed and cover the tabletops with snapshots. We display precious reminders.

Perhaps part of the way to a healthy balance between finding comfort in our remembrances and building a shrine comes in recognizing that there are seasons of remembering. Each season has its own level of need for and comfort derived from photographs and other keepsakes. Making the transitions between seasons can be awkward and painful, especially in a house where family members are in different places with their grief.

It's okay to display certain pictures, to leave rooms certain ways—for a time. And it's okay for those pictures to come down, or for a few to be weeded out. It's okay for steps to be taken, however small, that begin to turn the focus of your home to today and the future, not only the past.

There's no rush. But the day will come when it's time to start letting go by packing some things away, putting a fresh coat of paint on the walls—preparing for a future without the one you love, as painful as that may be.

Taking down a photo or turning a room back may not feel right. It may seem like erasing the reality and presence of the one we love—an erasing done with our own hand, by our own will.

But the time probably will be right at some point. To keep focusing intensely on your grief and on the one who has died is to refuse to open yourself up to those who are living around you, those who need you, and the future God has prepared for you.

WHAT DO YOUR REMEMBRANCES SAY?

It was a painful reality when I began to realize that photographs rather than mental images were defining my memories of Hope. It hurts when we begin to feel our memories slipping away, doesn't it?

Creating a scrapbook can help reverse the process and have a therapeutic, calming effect. It can become a creative outlet for grief in which you record memories of big events, ordinary conversations, funny things your loved one said or did, even annoying idiosyncrasies—and write them down while your recall is fresh. If scrapbooking isn't your style, you may want to put pictures and videos to music, including interviews with others who loved the one you've lost.

My friend Judy made a beautiful scrapbook of Hope's life for us. It's in a pretty, pink leather binder. After Gabe died, I bought a matching blue one and put together a scrapbook of his life.

These books are treasured stores of remembrance of the children I've lost. But they also taught me an important lesson about what our remembering says to family members who survive.

One day when we'd pulled the scrapbooks out for some reason, Matt looked at me and asked, "Where's mine?"

My quick answer was something like, "I don't have one for you because I have *you!*"

But his question penetrated me. I realized the pink and blue books said to him, "These children are special and valued and loved!" And there wasn't one for him. In my grief, I'd failed to celebrate in tangible ways the child I still had with me.

That became the launching point for "The Year of Matt"—a return to celebrating him, making sure I communicated to him in his love language that he is precious to me, enjoyed by me, enough for me. I needed to make sure that in the midst of all the attention and talking and writing about Hope and Gabe, Matt felt and knew that he is loved and enjoyed.

So I bought a black leather scrapbook, and on Matt's thirteenth birthday presented him with a book I'd made, "The Year of Being Twelve."

Every year since then, on his birthday, he's gotten another book or an update to his book celebrating the previous year. It's probably not the present he most looks forward to; when he turned 16, he no doubt would have preferred a car. But it's my way of letting him know that having him as our son is a joy to us, and that nothing— including the loss of his brother and sister—can take away from the happiness he brings.

Is there anything wrong with remembering someone we've lost? Of course not. But we're wise to ask ourselves some questions along the way:

- Am I preserving a memory or building a shrine?
- Is it time to put some things away, let some things go, and move our family focus to today and to the future?
- What does our home say to those who visit—and those who live here—about who we love and who we may have overlooked?

Chapter Twelve

The Grave

Nancy

We buried Hope in the warmth of June. A couple of weeks later I saw my friend Gigi, who had buried two children who'd died in her womb.

It was raining the day I saw her. Really raining. She told me how, since she'd buried her children, she had the maternal urge on rainy days to go to the cemetery and hold an umbrella over the grave to protect her babies from the soaking downpour.

I identified with her desire. A bit irrational, I know. But grief is not very rational—especially when it's fresh.

Then came that October morning when there was frost on the ground and a nip in the air and the heat came on for the first time, giving off the smell of burning dust. I lay in bed, feeling a wave of resistance and resentment toward the cold. I thought about how cold the ground was surrounding my precious daughter in the grave. I wept, wishing I could keep her body warm.

It's a mother's job to keep her child warm and protected, isn't it? That day I felt such a sense of helplessness in surrendering the body of my child to the coming winter.

Around that time, our neighborhood began the annual ritual of decorating for Halloween. When my neighbors hung their orange lights on October 1, it seemed a little early, but it was no big deal. I didn't want to be the Grinch of Halloween. I love a carved pumpkin, bales of hay, a few corncobs, and a silly costume. And I'm all for loading up on bite-size candy bars.

But then came the afternoon in late October when I drove through the neighborhood to pick up Matt from school. I passed a house showcasing a hearse with a casket coming out the back. A few doors down, several skeletons were hanging from trees.

It felt like a punch in the stomach.

In those days my thoughts were regularly running toward wondering about the decay of Hope's body in the grave. I was wondering how long it would take until there was little left except for bones.

So I felt assaulted by my neighbors' harmless hanging of skeletons in the trees. It seemed they were celebrating the very thing that brought me intense pain. I couldn't help wondering, *Have you ever had to bury someone you love?*

For the next few weeks, when I drove by, I did my best to look the other way.

DEALING WITH DEATH'S REALITIES

It seems everyone has his or her own way of handling facts and feelings about the body following death.

David, having spent four years living in a funeral home during college, came to believe that cremation is a wise way to go. That always made sense to me—until Hope died. I couldn't bear to think of burning up her body.

So we sought a beautiful place to bury her. I remember standing in the selected spot as the man from the cemetery explained that there would be room in the plot to bury another infant should we ever need to do so.

At the time I thought it was information we didn't need and would never use. But of course we did need it, and we did use it. Today there are two little bodies buried side-by-side in that plot, one marker for Hope and one for Gabriel.

In the weeks after putting Hope's body in the ground, I was

often drawn to make the 15-minute drive to that little plot in the country with its fresh sod trying and failing to take hold in the dry, dusty ground. I went on those unbearable days when I desperately wanted to feel close to her.

When I got there, though, I didn't know what to do or say, or how to act. I didn't know how long to stay. I felt as if a bait-and-switch had been pulled on me; I'd gone there longing to feel close to Hope, but it rarely worked out that way. Instead of relieving my pain, these visits merely punctuated it.

One day I was considering going to the grave and asked David if he wanted to go with me. I confessed to him my ambivalence in feeling drawn to go there and my steady experience of finding so little satisfaction in it.

"So then why do you feel you need to go?" he asked me.

After thinking for a moment, I realized what it was. "I don't want her to feel ignored by me," I said.

"Do you think Hope can feel ignored by you?" he asked gently.

"No, she can't."

That was the beginning of some freedom for me regarding the cemetery.

To Go or Not to Go

I still have an awkward relationship with the grave. But what freedom it brought to tell myself the truth: that Hope could not feel ignored by me. This dealt a blow to the false notion that my love for Hope was defined or demonstrated by frequent treks to the lonely place where her body is buried.

Since then, I've had some sweet times at the cemetery. I remember the day my friend Sue and I went there and spread out the beautiful quilt my grandmother made for Hope. We sat there with our Bibles open, working through my questions about whether or not Scripture supports the notion that babies who die go to heaven.[1]

I remember visiting the grave on the third anniversary of Hope's death, having just received my first copy of *Holding On to Hope*. What a bittersweet thing it was for David and Matt and me to thank God for the lasting impact of Hope's and Gabriel's lives as we held the book in our hands.

I recall going to the cemetery one day with my friend Marty. A man wandered over from visiting his wife's grave; he was so desperately lonely he couldn't stop talking. So we listened.

One Saturday morning on an anniversary of Hope's death, I took a group of friends who were helping me with *The One Year Book of Hope* by giving me input on what I was writing. We surrounded her gravestone with rose petals and wondered at the beauty together.

These and many others are sweet memories of that grave.

For a while a friend who has a loved one buried nearby would give me regular reports of the condition of Hope and Gabe's grave, telling me she had wiped away the dirt that had collected on the gravestone. I wondered whether she thought I should be more diligent about that.

I'm not a grave tender. I don't go often. I've released myself from the uncomfortable obligation. But neither am I a grave avoider.

Now when I go it's because I just want to—for the joy of remembrance on special days or ordinary days, the celebration of the lasting impact of Hope's and Gabe's lives, or sharing this important piece of myself with a new friend who wasn't in my life when we buried Hope and Gabe.

I recognize that many people experience a great deal of comfort and even a sense of companionship by visiting the grave of the one they love. For some, there's solace in the quietness and beauty and closeness they feel uniquely there. Perhaps that is you. You go to the grave to "talk" to the one who has died, to vent your frustrations and fears—but mostly to feel close. Many families like to decorate the grave on special days, or bring flowers—even a picnic. For many, visiting the grave is a cherished part of the healing process.

For the family whose loved one has been cremated, there may be no grave to visit. These families can find a place that brings them comfort and helps them feel close to the one they miss. Dedicating a tree or a garden bench, planting flowers or a grove of trees, or posting a plaque can help them honor their loved one's memory.

Visiting the grave can bring a sweet time of unity as families struggle to feel complete again. It can even be the impetus that helps a family heal and move forward. But other families find standing around the grave to be terribly awkward. Still others live with an enslaving compulsion toward the cemetery that keeps them from embracing each other—the living ones who need love. Constant grave visits can keep them so focused on death that they barely live.

This is different for every family, and for every family member. It can be awkwardly different at times, hard to talk about, even hard to accept. But we give each other a gift when we let each other deal with the grave's reality in his or her own way, in his or her own timing, making no demands and no judgments.

It's especially important to give our children a choice about visiting the grave. They may need several weeks or months to accept, process, and integrate the loss before facing the hard ground and the hard reality.

Perhaps the goal we should strive for is to be neither grave avoiders nor grave tenders. We can find that balance between remembering our loved ones in this way, in this location, and in remembering and celebrating them in other ways—ways that, for many family members, may be more joyful and less awkward.

OUR LITTLE PLOT OF LAND

David

Most men love to own a piece of real estate. I'm convinced it's encoded deep in our DNA. Watch us play Monopoly to get a clue to our hard-wired land-lust. Amassing property deeds, even fictitious ones, seems to fuel some primal urge to say, "Yes—I own that land!"

We derive some fundamental satisfaction in pointing to a piece of earth and saying to our wives, "See what I bought you, little lady?"

To our sons: "Someday, this will all be yours."

To our daughters: "You'll be safe here."

What irony for me the day I received my first wholly-owned, mortgage-free property deed. I was the proud owner of a four-foot-by-ten-foot plot of land in the community known as Harpeth Hills Memory Gardens. Nancy and I, knowing Hope's life would be short, had journeyed to the scenic country cemetery close to our home to buy a piece of land.

We gave no thought to resale value or the other usual concerns when choosing this property. The cemetery staff did try to point out the virtues of the plot we were eyeing: quiet end of the field, near trees, beautiful setting. But none of that really mattered to us. In fact, we felt very bewildered at the whole process.

How does one choose a good grave site? It seemed a bit bizarre to us to debate the features of different locations. Our baby daughter was dying. Were we really comparison-shopping for burial plots?

When we bought our house in Nashville, we thought it was cool that Goober from *The Andy Griffith Show* lived in our neighborhood. Should we now take some pride in Chet Atkins being a fellow resident of Harpeth Hills Memory Gardens?

Returning from the cemetery, I took my new property deed and filed it, with no pleasure. I didn't have the heart to even make a folder label for it; no pride of ownership on this one.

Nancy and I already had a different piece of real estate firmly in mind for Hope. We would have no choice but to commit her body to the ground at Harpeth Hills, but our true hope in the midst of this surreal property transaction was the strong and certain belief that a much more glorious destiny awaited her when she departed this earth.

She would obtain a home and inheritance that I could never

purchase for her. It was secured for her by Jesus Himself, who promised, "I am going there to prepare a place for you. . . . I will come back and take you to be with me that you also may be where I am" (John 14:2-3).

Paul affirms in 2 Corinthians 5:1, "Now we know that if the earthly tent we live in is destroyed, we have a building from God, an eternal house in heaven, not built by human hands."

Peter exults, "Praise be to the God and Father of our Lord Jesus Christ! In his great mercy he has given us new birth into a living hope through the resurrection of Jesus Christ from the dead, and into an inheritance that can never perish, spoil, or fade—kept in heaven for you" (1 Peter 1:3-4).

I don't often visit the grave of my children. Some may be surprised by that. I hope that doesn't make me an uncaring father. I find no real comfort there; it doesn't make me feel closer to them. I am occasionally drawn there to do little more than stop the rest of my life for a few moments and reflect on Hope's and Gabriel's lives, and the impact they had on mine.

Much more frequently, though, I think about their real home. I don't know what heaven is like. I know Jesus is there. I know that it is a place without pain, where our flawed little children find themselves complete, free from all of their many earthly limitations.

He who holds the keys to life and death holds the keys to the place prepared just for them. Fancifully, I imagine Him saying, "See what I bought for you? I told you someday it would all be yours! You'll be safe here."

FINDING HOPE BEYOND THE GRAVE

Nancy

Over the years, so many people have tried to comfort me by reminding me that Hope and Gabe are not in that grave—they're in heaven.

I know what those people are saying, and I believe it's true. But my children's bodies are in that grave, and I loved their bodies!

Their bodies are precious not only to me, but to God. Bodies must matter to God, because He'll use the seed of our earthly bodies to make new, glorified ones for us. Somehow He will take the matter that's been long buried or spread on the sea or in the wind and fashion it into something glorious—something fit for living with Him and reigning with Him in a new heaven and a new earth.

"And if the Spirit of him who raised Jesus from the dead is living in you, he who raised Christ from the dead will also give life to your mortal bodies through his Spirit, who lives in you" (Romans 8:11). Our greatest comfort at the grave is the truth that for those who know and love Christ, our final destiny is not the grave—it is glory. The grave is a brief resting place for this seed, this temporary tent called our mortal body.

One day God will infuse that seed with life. It will no longer be bound to the confines and coldness of the grave.

Sometimes it seems that day just won't come soon enough, doesn't it?

It helps me to know who is in charge of the grave. Giving the apostle John a glimpse of His glorified presence, Jesus says, "Do not be afraid! I am the First and the Last, and the Ever-living One. . . . I died, but see, I am alive forevermore; and I possess the keys of death and Hades (the realm of the dead)" (Revelation 1:17-18, AMP).

The person who holds the keys controls access, opens, and closes. As you face the emptiness and awkwardness of the cemetery, hear the promise found in the words of Jesus, who holds the keys of death and the grave. When the one you love died in that awful accident, it wasn't merely an accident. When the one you love died too soon, it was really right on time.

Jesus Himself controls life and death. That means you don't have to surrender the one you love to an unknown, uncaring nothingness. The person who knows Jesus is safely under His care and control.

As you stand by the grave, grab hold by faith to the promise of resurrection: "If all we get out of Christ is a little inspiration for a few short years, we're a pretty sorry lot. But the truth is that Christ has been raised up, the first in a long legacy of those who are going to leave the cemeteries. . . . It's resurrection, resurrection, always resurrection, that undergirds what I do and say, the way I live" (1 Corinthians 15:19-20, 32, MSG).

Chapter Thirteen

Going On

Nancy and David

As we come to the end of our conversation with you, we recognize that you have some very difficult choices ahead. You probably realize it, too.

In some ways, healing from the kind of loss you've experienced is like climbing a mountain. You keep having to do more hard things, and you wonder when you'll be able to coast through life again—when it will stop being so tough.

Life will never be what it was before your loss, but it can be good. Really good.

To get there, though, you have to make some difficult choices. You can't surrender to what comes naturally—which is giving in to grief as your new identity, living in the past, and giving up on life becoming good again.

GETTING UP

When she was twelve years old, our friend Peggy was walking along the road with her four-year-old sister—who was struck by a car and killed instantly.

Life as she knew it ended for Peggy that day, too.

Her mother was so devastated by the loss that the woman "took to the bed, and she rarely got up again," according to Peggy. From that day on, Peggy was on her own in a sense; her mother could not recover from her grief enough to make the most of still having Peggy.

When Peggy's mother died decades later, there was a huge indentation in her mattress—left by years of refusing to live in the face of death.

It's not that we are without sympathy. We understand the pull and pleasure of drawing up the covers in an effort to sleep away the pain that comes with loss. We understand the numbing effects of refusing to engage or to feel when feeling brings pain. But we also know that refusing to choose life means choosing to die—perhaps not physically, but emotionally and spiritually.

To choose life is to refuse to be enveloped by and eventually destroyed by heart-crushing sorrow and soul-stealing disappointment. To choose life is to keep turning toward God with all your heart and soul, so that He might replace the deadness inside you with His very own life and newness.

It is choosing to live fully for God, recognizing that there is no real life apart from Him and that anything less is merely existing. It's trusting God completely with your future and your family's future, knowing there may be even more loss ahead.

When we lose someone we love, we're faced with a cruel choice: give in to the weight of sorrow so that we get stuck and never move forward, or summon our energy and courage each morning to keep going and looking for brighter days.

Will you choose to get up—and keep getting up—and moving your family forward?

LETTING GO

About six months after Hope died, New Year's Day came around. On that day Nancy sat down to write in her journal:

January 1, 2000

It was a year ago I started writing this journal—the day I began chronicling our experience with Hope. But it seems so far away.

I've been trying to make the time to sit down over the holidays and bring some kind of conclusion to the journal—hoping something profound would hit me, some inspired wisdom, some dramatic send-off. I'm not looking for a neat and tidy ending, just meaningful.

But the truth is, I'm feeling rather numb these days. The lows are not quite so low, but the highs are not so high.

We just got back from a birthday gathering and in many ways I was back to my old self. I even casually told two people I met for the first time that I lost a daughter six months ago. No drama, no tears, and I'm wondering now if they think I barely care.

I asked David a few days ago if he is tired of my being sad. "Yes," he answered honestly. Part of me wanted to scream out at him, but I'm sure it must be a drag, at times, to live with someone who is so sad. But how can I stay close to her if I don't stay sad? Sometimes I want to scream because I feel so torn.

When they told us Hope was going to die, I accepted it pretty quickly and dealt with the reality of it throughout the months. But now I feel so frustrated that I don't have a daughter.

Sometimes when I say that I wish Hope was here, David is quick to remind me how sick she was. And I know he is right. I guess what I really want is a healthy Hope, here, now, growing, smiling, walking, catching everyone's attention with her charm.

I'm rambling. Nothing profound to say. No real closure. Not even spiritual summation.

Dear Hope:

We've just entered a new century. Everyone is relieved that Y2K was not a disaster and excited about what the future holds. But I don't want it to be another year. It just takes me further away from you.

*And I want so desperately to feel close to you, to be able to hear
you in my mind even if all I ever got to hear from you was a cry. I
want to feel your skin and stroke your cheek. I want to wake up and
find you here.*

*But you are so far away and becoming even more distant in my
memory and it is so painful.*

*And I feel weak. I used to feel strong—when you were here and
in the months after you left—I hurt but I felt strong spiritually, emotionally. Now I just feel numb and weak and lacking in purpose.*

*I don't know how to let you go and hold on to you at the same
time. I don't know how to feel the pain and embrace joy at the same
time.*

*I loved you, Hope. I love you now. And I can hardly wait to see
you again.*

*Forgive me for going on with life without you. Forgive me for
forgetting what you sound like and what you looked like and what it
felt like to spend the morning in bed with you on my chest. It just
keeps moving farther and farther away.*

There comes a time in our grief that we realize we have to figure out how to keep on living, how to incorporate the loss into our
lives. We want to feel normal again, to feel joy again. But even enter-
taining that prospect feels like a betrayal of the person who is gone.

While the constant remembering, thinking about, and crying
over the one we miss is exhausting, that energy and emotion of grief
keep us feeling close to the one we love. And we're so desperate to
feel close. Beginning to let go of our grief feels like letting go of the
one we love, leaving him or her behind and moving on. The very
idea is unbearable.

It is a cruel choice to have to make. It feels completely unfair,
but unavoidable. We can either hold on to the pain, accepting its
regular doses of misery because it keeps us connected to the loved

one we've lost—or we can choose to release it, process it, talk about it, cry about it, let it wash over us, and then let it wash away with our tears.

We can make the painful choice to let it go—not all at once, but a little every day. We find that we can decide whether or not to let ourselves sink to that place where the flashes of memories and reminders of loss threaten our contentment and composure.

We can begin to make that hard choice. We can begin to let go of our grief so we can grab hold of life and those who are living.

But the only way we can do that is by telling ourselves the truth: If we choose to let go of the pain, or at least let it become manageable, it doesn't mean we love the one we've lost any less. And it doesn't mean that person's life was any less significant or meaningful, or that we will forget.

Letting go hurts, takes time, and need not be rushed. But it shouldn't be avoided altogether. We feel the pain, mourn the loss, shed our tears, and with time can begin to let go of the grief that's had such a hold on us.

Perhaps it's not so much that we let go of our grief, but that we give our grief permission to lessen its grip on us. Will you give your grief permission to loosen its grip on you and your family?

GOING ON

We put off taking a family photo for about a year and a half after Hope died. When we finally sat down under the tree in the park with the photographer giving us directions, it was all we could do to smile. We were painfully aware that this would not be a picture of our whole family—that we would never again have a photograph of our complete family.

We would never have dreamed at that point that healing could bring us to the place where we are today—with our family of three enjoying life together. We know the day is coming when our family of five will be together. We're aware that Hope and Gabe are separated from us, but that awareness no longer has the power to rob us of our joy in having each other and living life together.

That is what we wish for you, as you face the days ahead—that you and your family will smile at the future together with thanks to God for how He has met you in this hard place. May you have a sense of anticipation about how He is going to use your loss in your own lives, and in the lives of those around you, for good.

Right now it may feel like something has been taken from you that reduces and limits and hurts your family. But as God brings healing, your family will experience increasing gratitude—for how the one you loved, and even the process of losing that person, has not reduced you but expanded and enriched you.

Your loss has given you a new appreciation for life—and a new anticipation of eternity.

Notes

Chapter 5

1. © 2001 Simpleville Music (ASCAP). All rights administered by Simpleville Music, Inc. Words and music by Bart Millard. All rights reserved. Used by permission.

Chapter 6

1. The Compassionate Friends, "The Death of a Child," June 1999, and "When a Child Dies: A Survey of Bereaved Parents," October 2006.
2. David Popenoe, Barbara Dafoe Whitehead, "The State of Our Unions 2007: The Social Health of Marriage in America," The National Marriage Project, Rutgers University, July 2007.

Chapter 12

1. As we worked through the Bible that day, I became convinced that Scripture teaches the comforting truth that babies are welcomed lovingly into heaven. But I was helped even more a few years later when I read John MacArthur's book *Safe in the Arms of God: Truth from Heaven About the Death of a Child* (Thomas Nelson, 2003).

FREE Discussion Guide!
A reproducible version of this book's
discussion questions is available at:

ChristianBookGuides.com